If Aristotle Ran the Catholic Church

The Present Leadership Problem of the Church

By

William L. Forst

© 2004 by William L. Forst. All rights reserved.

No part of this book may be reproduced, stored in a retrieval system, or transmitted by any means, electronic, mechanical, photocopying, recording, or otherwise, without written permission from the author.

ISBN: 1-4140-0531-8 (e-book)
ISBN: 1-4140-0530-X (Paperback)
ISBN: 1-4140-0529-6 (Dust Jacket)

This book is printed on acid free paper.

1stBooks - rev. 03/25/04

Prologue

I dedicate this book to my parents both of whom are dead. Dad (Frank) died of an accident December 11, 1940; I was 12 years of age. My Mother (Bertha) who somehow continued their support died June 12, 1966. Both parents gave me the practical side of leadership. They were Servant leaders as Jesus described.

I wish to express appreciation of my eight siblings, all of whom are alive, I being the youngest at 75. Each of the eight is an independent character, and I value the manner in which we challenge one another. We all belong to the same religion - sort of - Roman Catholic, even though many are Republican and I a Democrat with my parents. The challenge of my family is a constant push for me to change and grow, however not always do I grow in the direction some members wish.

I have been writing and rewriting this book for six years. I will be glad to see it in print, so that I will no longer be able to change it. The process of writing has given me a crack at creativity and imagination I never experienced before.

I appreciate the support I have received from my classmates who meet each month. They are Jim Cahalin, Frank Gillgannon, Bill Lally, Tom Mullen, Bo Ryan, and the deceased Charles Pfeiffer. The ability to state one's case, and know that one will be listened to and also vehemently questioned without being condemned as a heretic, is a great support to me. This is how new ideas are born. We need a great number of new ideas in our country and church today.

Also very special help from my niece Jeanne and her husband David Robertson. Dave gave me a needed critique on the first edition. This helped me to assign it to the waste can. After a year there was a resurrection. I changed it around, put some order to it, and it worked out to the present reading.

I have written my autobiography (not printed yet) in which I describe my personal experience of the many styles of leadership described in this book. Jesus asked for Servant Leadership. Since Vatican II (1965) Servant Leadership is the way, but it will be many years before we rid ourselves of the Lord and Master style. May Vatican II leadership be our future?

Thanks much for the beautiful ride of life.
Bill Forst

The Church will have to make a big jump of faith

Contents

Prologue .... **iii**
Introduction .... **vii**
Chapter # 1 .... **1**
   The Intellect is Nourished by Truth... 1
   Truth demands Trust 8
   Truth and Trust must struggle with Power.................................. 12
   The Intellect makes itself secure in Patriarchy 20
   Truth is Disfigured by Deception 26
   The Intellect's Search for Truth Demands Continual Change 33
   From Truth Equality most follow 40

Chapter # 2 .... **45**
   Aesthetics is directed toward Beauty 45
   Creativity-Imagination is the bedrock of Aesthetics..................... 50
   Aesthetics is Beauty through Networking 57
   The Feminine is at the Heart of Aesthetics 62
   Aesthetics as Diversity, Diversity as Beauty 70

Chapter # 3 .... **73**
   Moral is attracted to Goodness 73
   Goodness as Ethics 74
   Prophecy the Core of the Moral 77
   Moral Act Requires Freedom 83
   Moral Recognizes Human Dignity 90
   The Morality and Goodness of a Franchise Parish 91
   Moral as Related to Law... 97

Chapter # 4 .... **103**
   The Spiritual generates Unity 103

Unity within Diversity 107
Unity as uniqueness 117
Spirituality as Listening Brings Unity 123
Spirituality is Friendship 126
Spirituality Makes the Servant Leader.................................... 130
Servant Leader Evokes Community 133
Spirituality is Our Work 138
Conclusion..**142**
Bibliography **153**
Index..**157**
About the Author..**163**

The future is bright

Introduction

This book is about leadership - leadership in the Roman Catholic Church, and the basic leadership designed by Jesus. Jesus called this leadership **Servant, Shared**, or **Partner**. There is no place in the gospels where Jesus sanctions a monarchical, patriarchal, dominating, or dictatorial type of leadership.

"Caution is everywhere, courage is nowhere, and soon we shall all die of prudence"
Cardinal Leo Josef Suenens

Some folks have asked me: by what authority do I write such a book? My response is that I have a great deal of experience being on the receiving end of leadership. I have experienced *'What are the good benefits of a Servant Leader'* and I have greater familiarity with *'How NOT to Lead'*. In the midst of this I know what I like. I like to be treated as a dignified human being, with a good deal of pastoral experience, at times much more experience that my leaders. I know from the gospels the kind of leadership that Jesus fostered and encouraged. Jesus said a leader a is person who is able to do the most menial task in the institution; washing the feet of the others, regarding oneself as the least. Servant leader is a person who cares for the outcasts of the community. For Jesus **servant leadership** is possible for all institutions; business, church, state, etc. It seems improbable to be able to find out how to lead from the people who are in leadership positions, unless they have come from the bottom. Many of our leaders in church or state have NOT the experience of being the outcast or the least. In modern times Nelson Mandela of South Africa is one of these leaders.

I have never been in a position of high leadership within the church, even though I have a brother a Bishop and another brother a Monsignor. However I have been pastor of several parishes. I was principal of a high school seminary, organizer and co-director of the Jefferson City Diocese Social Concern (Catholic Charities). As co-director with Sr. Pat Moix, I accredit that she brought servant leadership to our small 'curia post'. Pat was educated in psychology and demonstrated how important are the 4 dimensions of human development. I have done years in prison work where I came up against some very dysfunctional leadership. Finally I spent a couple of years among the very poor in Peru. One can learn servant leadership in living with and being among the poor. This is the closest I got to being poor.

Leadership in any institution has a lot to do with how one understands authority. The Greek word *exousia* = authority, and its meaning as it appears in the Gospels is **'Strength of character'** **'act as oneself'**, and **'in sense of ability'**. Authority is a relationship word; it does not happen because of a 'high' position given to a person. Authority happens when a relationship enables and entices a person to use the gifts of creativity and imagination God has given them. This happens when authority functions within freedom. Such authority will of necessity be shared, or partnered, or as Jesus indicated it will be **Servant**. Servant authority exists only in a loving relationship. The servant leads by enabling others to use and perform their skills. The servant leader permits others the freedom to fully respond to God's Spirit.

Jesus is the prime example of this Servant leadership, and he asked his followers to lead as he does. Jesus said: Lk. 22: 24-27, *"the greatest among you must become like the youngest, and the leader like one who serves."* Jesus indicated that leaders must wash the feet of those served - Jn 13: 8-14, *"So if I, your Lord and Teacher, have washed your feet, you also ought to wash one another's feet."* These are powerful and revolutionary words and practice coming from Jesus. I agree with Larry Rasmussen when he writes,

> *"His is an upside-down kingdom whose ways contrast with those of 'kings' and 'benefactors'. In His reign, he tells them, status distinctions are reversed."*[1]

Would it not be refreshing and hope filled if a person appointed Bishop (Or Pope) in his acceptance speech would say,

> **"I am not your Lord and Master. I will discontinue the traditions of Master rule, such as dress, title, and living**

---

[1] Ann Pederson, "God, Creation, and All That Jazz", Chalice Press, St. Louis, MO. 2001 Also Larry Rasmussen, "Shaping Communities," Ed. Dorothy C. Bass, (San Francisco: Jossey-Bass, 1997) 121

style. I am not your King. I intend to be Servant, I intend to wash the feet of the people of this diocese."

We can presume that servant leadership **guided the early church**. However as the church grew remote from Jesus and his times, the leadership changed. A drastic change in leadership style came to the church in 313 AD with the **Edict of Milan**. The Emperor took over the church, and 'Caesar became Pope'. This was good for the church in that persecutions would be eliminated, and the church was given legal status. It also was very destructive for the church with the new style of leadership. The church took on the form of leadership of its captors. Historians today refer to this leadership born in the church as **'Monarchial Bishoprics'**. The leaders in the church acted like 'little kings'; they dressed like kings, they lived like kings, they ruled like kings-with infallible power, and they conducted liturgical gatherings as kings. From this early time to the present there has been a constant battle between **servant vs. patriarchal** type of leadership, or leadership that is **shared vs. dictatorial**. There were many Popes who attempted to lead the church as servant leaders. There were many more who gave in to the pure pleasure of power and ruled by dominating and dictatorial leadership. The meaning of **'power corrupts and absolute power corrupts absolutely'** becomes very evident.

100 years before World War II the leadership in the Church was a disaster. In 1959 the Cardinals elected the small chubby **Pope John XXIII**. Pope John called the Vatican II council in 1962. He

attempted to bring the church into the type of leadership that Jesus first taught - that of shared and servant leadership. He would be successful in bringing this about, at least in the documents of the Council. The documents called for collegiality and subsidiarity in church leadership. **Collegial** meant that leadership must be shared, and **Subsidiarity** saw that leadership would not be dominated from the top. These are two simple Christian ideals which, in 1965, ushered in a Copernican revolution in leadership within the church. Even though a majority of Bishops voted for this revolution, it became very difficult to erase the past practice. One result was a great exodus (1960-1970s) of middle management (priests and bishops) from the church. One estimate is; that 100,000 priests and bishops worldwide removed themselves from the priesthood, and possibly about 30,000 priests and bishops here in the United States. It was the greatest and most sudden depletion of middle management personnel the church has ever seen. People give many reasons for this, but high on the reckoning is a failure of **servant-shared leadership.** One difficulty with the Vatican II documents is that so many compromises had to be made, and every compromise weakened the teaching. These compromises are haunting the present church and Pope John Paul II.

Cardinal Suenens quote *"Caution is everywhere, courage is nowhere, and soon we shall all die of prudence"* applies today. Today we have leaders who are micromanagers and co-dependent; who express no trust for those 'below' them. They only trust those 'above'. They seek control, and that brings on secrecy and deception; thus truth is sacrificed. The people realize the lack of truth, and this spells distrust, the church is spinning madly in this circle today. One reason for this circle is that church leaders have never had the privilege of being trained in the seminary in servant leadership, or in management nor has it been thought necessary to teach it after ordination. And so the circle of mismanagement continues unabated.

> *"Those who know the truth are not equal to those who love it, and they who love it are not equal to those who delight in it."*
>
> Confucius

Cicero (106-43 BC), a philosopher and orator, living at the time of Jesus, described Socrates (470-399 BC) as the first man ever to bring philosophy into the marketplace. Plato (428 - 348 BC) a student of Socrates expanded upon his teacher's philosophy. Finally Aristotle came on the scene (384 - 322 BC), a student of Socrates and Plato, **Aristotle** searched deeply into human nature. Aristotle brings us the beginnings of democracy based upon respecting the dignity of the human. With Aristotle we also have the beginnings of Servant Leadership. **Jesus**, living 300 hundred years after Aristotle, enhanced and updated Aristotle's concept of the human being as God's Image. Jesus also improved the idea of servant leadership within democracy. Aristotle is the chief proponent of the four dimensions of human experience.

In the following chapters I plan on calling upon Aristotle, the prophets of old, and many wise men and women in history to point out the type of leadership the church needs in order to carry out the mission of Jesus to the world. It does not matter who you are a single, married, employed, unemployed, priest, minister, bishop, mother, president, CEO, prisoner, electrician, etc, whatever our duty and position is in the world, we will find fulfillment, contentment, satisfaction in living the four basic dimensions of life.

Jesus was no doubt familiar with Greek culture and had some knowledge of Aristotle and other Greek Philosophers. The four basic dimensions of Aristotle fit right into Jesus thought and can be realized in the many parables and stories he told.

The four dimensions are:

Chapter #1 - ***The Intellectual is nourished by Truth.*** Truth in all matters (even sexual) is the prime concern for a Servant Leader. Truth generates trust in and for the People of God. Truth and trust 'wash the feet' of the people and this defeats the addiction to patriarchic power. Truth finds there is no need for deception and secrecy. A result of this is equality among all sexes.

Chapter #2 - ***The Aesthetic is directed toward Beauty.*** A servant leader will advance the cause of aesthetics. Aesthetics will flourish when God's gifts of imagination and creativity function freely. God's Spirit comes to us through creativity. Aesthetics will find methods of networking with the amazing diversity that exists in

God's creation. The feminine is a very important expression of aesthetics. Aesthetics brings out the beauty of ritual (liturgical) engendering activity rather than passivity.

Chapter #3 - ***The Moral is attracted to Goodness*** Good ethical standards must include prophecy. The human being is respected and develops moral goodness in an atmosphere of freedom, and in the framework of law. We take a serious look at the morality of the developing franchise parish (as/or business), and ask, "Is this moral?"

Chapter #4 - ***The Spiritual generates Unity.*** Spirituality of a Servant leader engenders unity among religions, which in turn brings peace. Spirituality will bring unity where there is diversity, and acceptance where there is uniqueness. The servant leader encourages tolerance, justice, and acceptance within a plurality of people worldwide. The end work of spirituality is living as community. I believe firmly that Servant Leadership is a critical importance for the Catholic Church today. Without this leadership the church will find it impossible to lead the third millennium.

A final word of appreciation to Tom Morris[2] who is a philosopher and has taught for many years at Notre Dame University. He wrote a book, **"If Aristotle Ran General Motors,"** using the wisdom of the philosophers of the past, and applied their insights to running big business. Morris was always concerned with the dignity

---

[2] Tom Morris, "If Aristotle Ran General Motors", (Henry Holt and Company, N.Y.) 1997

of the human being. This is certainly the main point of the four dimensions. I received great inspiration from Tom Morris' work.

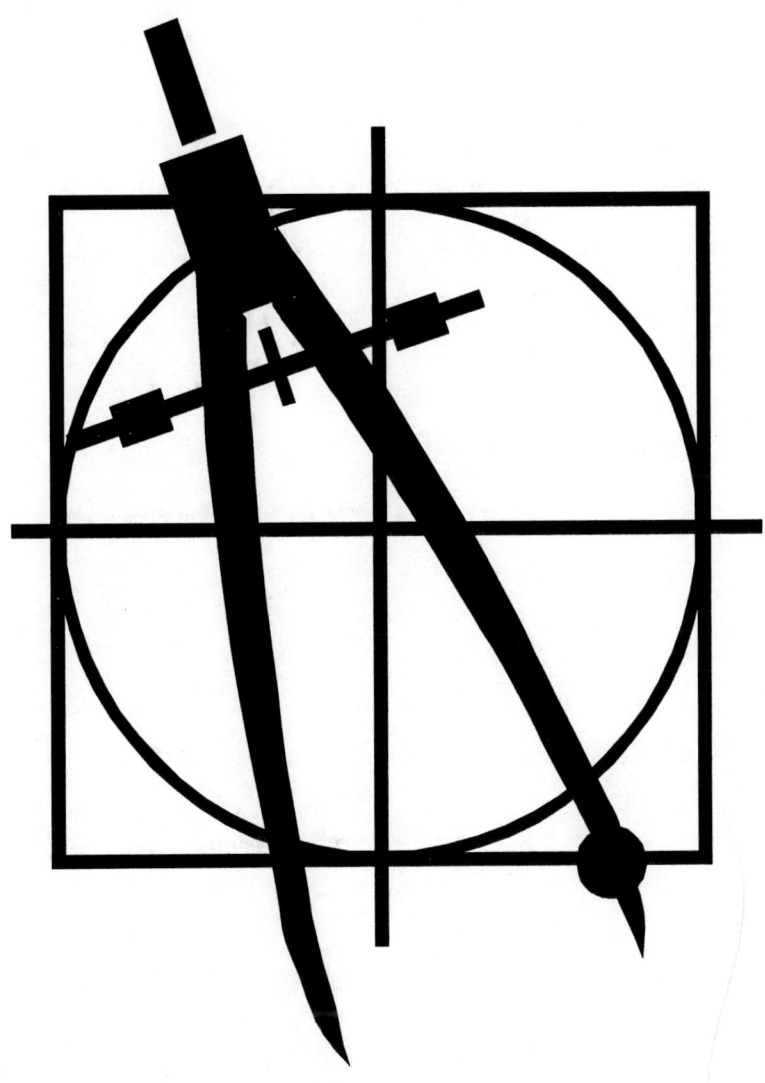

The Church is Global and finding its way

Chapter #1

The Intellect is Nourished by Truth – p. 1
Truth Demands Trust – p. 8
Truth and Trust must struggle with Power – p. 12
The intellect makes itself secure in Patriarchy – p. 20
Truth is Disfigured by Deception – p. 26
The Intellect's Search for Truth Demands Continual Change – p. 33
From Truth Equality most follow – p. 40

The Intellect is Nourished by Truth

"When you invite people to think you are inviting revolution" Ivone Gebrara

"Such is the irresistible nature of truth that all it asks, and all it wants, is the liberty of appearing." Thomas Paine

Aristotle wrote about truth in contrast to falsehood in this manner: *"To say of what is that it is not, or of what is not that it is so, is false; while to say of what is so that it is so, and what is not so that it is not so, is true."* From the beginning of the world we know that the object of the intellect is truth, for Genesis 1:27, says *"God created humankind in his image."* Our God is a God of truth; we are to image that truth. Jesus spent his time testifying to the truth. In the 8th chapter of John's gospel, Jesus argues, with the religious professionals of his day, about who he is, and what is the truth, and

William L. Forst

finally Jesus says: v. 32 ***"If you continue in my word, you are truly my disciples, and you will know the truth, and the truth will make you free."*** In John 18:37-38 during Jesus' trial, Jesus indicated that he was a person of truth and Pilate gives us his amazing question, "***What is the truth?***" This question is as relevant today, in and out of the Church, as it was at the time of Jesus.

God has given humans the beautiful gift of intellect. The intellect works well with two other gifts of God, which are **creativity** and **imagination**. All three gifts are unique to us as human beings, and they function most properly in freedom. Freedom is like water to a fish, the gifts of the human being cannot be fully realized unless the intellect is "swimming" in freedom. We Christians believe that when we are swimming in this freedom (Rom 8:21) our gifts of imagination and creativity become vibrant and alive. We believe that in this freedom we contact and respond to the Spirit of God (2 Thess 5:19), and it is with God's Spirit that we come upon truth. Jesus called his Apostles and Disciples to Servant leadership. The leadership's work is to present the truth *"that will make you free."* This is true of the Church in Jesus' day, and it is true today. Today the church is global, bureaucratic, a highly structured caste system. Margaret Wheately[3] says such a large system (General Motors or church) is able to maintain itself only when it encourages great amounts of individual freedom.

---

[3] Margaret J. Wheately, "Leadership and the New Science". Berrett-Koehler Pubs. San Francisco, 1999 p.xvi

To serve people well, whether as parent, priest, educator, bishop, business manager or pope, there is nothing more important than the truth. Truth is indispensable in human being's search for happiness. Confucius said, *"Those who know the truth are not equal to those who love it, and they who love it are not equal to those who delight in it."* Confucius is saying that truth is not only rational, as is stated in the Nicean creed, but truth is emotional, empathetic, and understanding. In fact truth will involve the other three dimensions: Aesthetics, Moral, and Spiritual.

The search for truth is ever-changing as I write. In the past the pursuit of truth was pretty much centered around a dominating leader (father, CEO, pope, educator), normally male (patriarchy). The truth functioned within the political, spiritual, and economic venue. Order was brought about by imposing control and restricting freedom (hierarchy). The physics of Sir Isaac Newton gave scientific support to this system of old. The truth was obtained and dispensed in a mechanistic and deterministic fashion. Truth came from cause and effect. Change, in such a system, was considered unacceptable, or at least unnecessary. In addition those receiving the truth had to accept it without any questions (blind obedience).

The leadership of the Catholic Church at the time of the Protestant Reformation protected the **"truth"** from error (Protestant). Error has no rights. In the 1500s, the Council of Trent, there appeared a new seminary system, wherein the church developed a compliant, submissive and controlled clergy. The clergy responded to **"command and order"**. There was no free conscience, no freedom of religion, and no respect for human dignity. In the midst of all of this the Catholic Church developed a celebrated caste system to retain control (hierarchy). This control functions even today. With this system the church had a very clear, precise, flow of information that was called **"truth"**. This dominating system reached its peak with the reign of Pope Pius IX, Vatican Council I (1870), and Infallibility. Nothing was really done about this dominating system - through two world wars - until Vatican Council II (1962). Now the ***"The truth will set you free."***

Today, there is a distinct search for the truth. This search for truth is based on love, relationship, and the dignity of the human being. It is not new, for many philosophers, mystics, and Jesus taught it years ago. The new search for truth turns around Jesus' command ***"love the neighbor as oneself."*** It embraces the pluralism of the global society. As with Jesus this search for truth is inclusive. There are those who argue the present search for truth springs out of what is being experienced in the new science.

Quantum physics has all of creation in the universe in relationship. Relationship determines all that is created by God, even the subatomic world. Donella Meadows[4] quoted an ancient Sufi (Moslem teacher) that captured the dynamic shift between the new and the old,

---

[4] Margaret Meadows, "Whole Earth Models and Systems." Co-Evolution Quarterly (Summer 1982): 98-108

"You think because you understand 'one' you must understand 'two,' because one and one makes two. But you must also understand 'and".

The new science is what Margaret J. Wheatley[5] calls ***autopoiesis***, an old Greek term, which simply means that living systems can create, and renew its own. Scientists call it **self-organization** and the **self-referencing** ability of the species. What this means is that in the process of evolution the species (subatomic as well) have the ability to know itself, to know what it is supposed to do, to adapt to the new. It is not locked into a certain structure. It is capable of organizing into whatever form it determines best suits the present situation. It is different from the Newtonian arrangement (the old science or system). The new science the specie has a desire and drives to know and understand itself. Present within the intelligence of the species is a dynamic search for truth. The species will seek out organization and order. The amazing thing is this order will come out of disorder and chaos. The presence of chaos is the indication of new life. The old system (Newtonian) feared any change, for change brought disorder and chaos. Order is brought by imposing control and restricting freedom. For Christians, chaos is the crucifixion; order came out of this chaos with the resurrection. The resurrection was radically new, the chaos of the crucifixion was conquered, and freedom and truth came forth. The new science says it is NOT possible to bring new life while restricting freedom and creativity. It is in freedom that the species find their way and organize for growth

---

[5] Ibid Margaret J. Wheatley, p. 20.

and change. For us as Christians, it is in this freedom that our imagination and creativity receive the Spirit of God.

Margaret J. Wheatley[6] beautifully weaves a picture of leadership in the pursuit of truth. Even though she doesn't use the word "servant", it is the same servant leadership that Jesus demanded from his followers. It is as though the new science is fully agreeing with Jesus in his pursuit of truth, or even Aristotle in his democratic process. The *'autopoiesis'* is advocating that the human being is created to the image of God. We humans, as "Image of God', have the gifts of intelligence, free will, creativity and imagination. With these gifts we are able to "**self-organize**" and we have the ability to "**self reference**" as does all of creation. These gifts can only operate in freedom, and it is in freedom that we contact the Spirit of God. The Church cannot restrict the freedom of the People of God, the church cannot restrict access to the Spirit of God, and the church cannot force, control, or manipulate the disclosure of faith by the People of God.

Where the Newtonian science mandated control and restricted freedom to arrive at order and the "truth", the new science permits freedom and ventures into chaos and disorder. The new system has trust in the human dignity and perceives that a new beginning, a resurrection, a new truth, will come out of chaos, as it did in the 1st chapter of Genesis, as it did in Vatican II. The old order fears freedom while the new order embraces freedom. The old leaders led by force,

---

[6] Ibid

control, domination, and manipulation. The new leadership is based on relationship and equality among people, it believes in the goodness of the human being. The old system emphasizes original sin while the new system gives credence to original justice and the grace of God. The leaders of the old system are called 'Supreme', 'King', 'God', 'Infallible', and 'all knowing'. In the new system the leaders are called 'Servant', 'Partner,' and 'Helpmate', for they are willing to 'wash the feet' of the People of God. The old system determined the 'truth' for the sheep. The New system searches with the sheep for the 'truth', with the help of the Spirit of God, and believes the *'truth will set you free'*.

There are those today who feel the Church has moved away from the truth presented in Vatican II council of the 1960's. Enough to read the recent book by Garry Wills[7] where he speaks of *'structures of deceit'* in the church. When any organization builds upon structures of deceit then it is true that the leadership is not in pursuit of truth. Deceit and truth are like water and oil and they do not mix. A good example of deceit and secrecy vs. truth is the priest and bishop pedophile scandal of 2002. The bishops used secrecy and deceit (scandal of 2001) to avoid exposing the truth of the weakness and addiction of the clergy. In this game of manipulation they have paid off victims of sexual abuse to keep them quiet. Thus the victim becomes victim twice. This is deceit and the absence of the truth. This game should never be played at any price and for any purpose,

---

[7] Garry Wills, "Papal Sin" (Doubleday, NY) 2000

sexual, political, or in any of the many dealings of the church. The fact that most of this deceit was done in innocence by the bishops (it is just the way we do it), is the greatest argument that we have that indicates a drastic systemic change in the church is needed. The truth will make us free. *"Consecrate them by means of truth—'Your word is truth'* **(Jn 17:17).**

Truth demands Trust

"The objects of the heart are truth and justice"
Thomas Aquinas.
**Truth is a passion of the heart. Truth is a heart issue -
Its quest is justice.**

Most philosophers indicate that truth is the basis for trust. Christianity lives to observe Jesus' command, ***"Love the neighbor as oneself."*** This can only be done in and with relationships that are built on trust. To have effective and competent interpersonal relations we have to have trust. However, the question always is, ***"How do you build trust in one's leaders?"*** A leader can be your pastor, a parent, a boss, a teacher, a pope, a president, or a scoutmaster. For most of us this trust comes when we know our leader, and this knowing is based on personally being in touch with our leaders. In today's culture and society and with the presence of high tech communications and big bureaucracies, it becomes increasingly impossible to know our leaders, or for the leaders to know those whom they lead. In such an atmosphere trust can be difficult to generate.

In today's culture and society it is almost impossible for a leader (pope, president, pastor) to have the immediate trust of those who are lead. Confucius understood that just being in a position of leadership did not make a leader. Jesus, on many occasions, indicated the same (Mt 20:25). The truth of ones leadership has to be the very core of the leader. The leader has to love it, live it and even delight in it. All of this has to be experienced by the lead. So the equation is true, that the closer we are personally to our leader, the better we know him/her as a person, and the more we are able to share ideas, the more trust we will have in the leader. When we are not able to personally know our leader, if the leader is not in touch with the followers, then the trust level is weakened. I recently asked a pastor of a large parish with 3500 families (something over 10,000 people), *"With how many parishioners do you have some personal relationship? Would it be around half."* He said, *"Are you kidding? I may know by sight somewhere around half, but a personal relationship with very few - maybe 10% (350)".* The 10% may be even far too ambitious.

People are not machines, and people will reject being treated as a machine, even when this happens in a church setting. One of the most ennobling gestures a leader, parent or priest can make toward another person is to ask her, *"what do you think about—?"* This presumes that the person is able to think, is able to have some ideas, that she has an opinion, and that she knows something about what you are saying. This gives respect to that person. The person responds with trust. If people do not know their pastor, can there be much trust present?

I filled in for a pastor who had vacated his parish for a sabbatical. We had weekday masses. At the homily time I made a very brief explanation and clarification of the scripture readings, and then I said, **"What do you think about—?"** At first the people were dumb, but then they got used to it, and even liked it. I wanted to know what they thought, and I wanted to show that I respected their thoughts. The result was a beautiful challenging dialogue. They began to trust me, when it appeared that I was not correcting them, or indicating to them that they were wrong. They trusted me when I respected them in our mutual search for the truth. After a couple of weeks a lady came up to me after Mass and said, **"Your little dialogue after the gospel - it is like you trust that I have something to say".** She said she felt very good about this, she felt important, and anticipated attending the weekday Masses. We were all interested in seeking the truth. We were all seeking to respond to the Spirit of God. To do this we all had to respect and trust one another.

Gary Zukav[8] tells a story of a figure ice skating couple. The beauty and grace with which they skated. Sometimes she in front of him and other times she leading him, moving at breakneck speeds. At times she, in a very defenseless position, is raised high over his head, with the ice below as hard as concrete. The rapid movements are done with utmost precision and grace. Their skill, strength, and

---

[8] Gary Zukav, "Soul Stories", Simon & Schuster, NY, 2000 p. 211-214

creativity kept all folks on the edge of their seat. Indeed it is a expression of rare beauty. They utterly delight in one another. Each provides the freedom to the other, so each may come to their full potential. They can only do this because they **trust** one another. This similar excitement might happen within our religion. The disciples having the freedom to use the strengths and talents, to arrive at their potential. They are to work with one another as partners, meshing their strengths and weakness into a beautiful performance. Responding to the Spirit of God. When the talents and gifts of each are combined and partnered, then *"In God everything is possible"*. However many of the religions today seem to be interested in control (and money) rather than enticing their members to freely respond to God's Spirit.

Trust and truth cannot be separated. These two are separated when leaders are imposed upon the people without the people's consent. This amounts to distrust for the people - **'you are not educated enough to choose your own leader.'** When the leader is appointed, s/he must then earn the trust of the people. This may take a month, a year, or it may never occur. When people are permitted to have 'advise and consent' concerning their leaders, they generally choose leaders who they know are truthful. When a leader is approved of by the people, the leader receives trust from the people. This leader cannot govern without trust.

Case at hand the Bishops meeting in Dallas TX June 2002, Bishop Wilton Gregory spoke the following prophet words:

William L. Forst

> *"The crises (scandal), in truth, is about a profound loss of confidence by the faithful in addressing the crime of the sexual abuse of children and young people by priests and church personnel......Only by truthful confession, heartfelt contrition and firm purpose of amendment can we hope to receive the generous mercy of God the forgiveness of our brothers and sisters."[9]*

We wait and see if contrition and reform comes. When people lose trust in their Bishop (Law of Boston) the leader must leave.

Jesus expressed trust in his disciples on many occasions. (Jn 6:60-67) The disciples said *"Who can accept it?"* of the teaching of Jesus about the eating of his body and blood. Jesus indicated that he knew it was difficult to believe. He did not threaten or force anyone, and many indicated that they would not believe. They lost trust in Jesus. Jesus did not force his disciples, for he trusted them. Jesus said to his disciples, *"Do you also wish to go away?"* They trusted Jesus; they did not leave.

Truth and Trust must struggle with Power

Power corrupts, absolute power corrupts absolutely - Lord Acton

Nietzsche says of power,

> *"Not necessity, nor desire - no, the love of power is the demon of men. Let them have everything - health, food, a place to live, entertainment - they are and remain unhappy*

---

[9] St. Louis Post Dispatch, News, Friday June 14, 2002 p. A6

and low spirited: for the demon (power) waits and waits and will be satisfied." [10]

Power appears to be an intellectual thing, as power is presently used by many businesses, churches and other organizations. Power has very little to do with aesthetics, morality, or spirituality. As an intellectual thing, it has much to do with the left-brain activity. This type of power is principally a 'man' thing as Nietzsche seems to indicate.

Power is very addictive. I suspect power is more addictive than any substance addiction. Strong power **"gets what it wants"**, it states, **"I am the one who makes the decisions"**, it rules according to **"might makes right"**. Addictive power has a need to **"trample on the rights and needs of others"**. The old saying that was made famous by Lord Acton at the time of Vatican Council I (1870), ***"power corrupts, absolute power corrupts absolutely"*** is still true. The history of the Church, past and present, proves the addictiveness of power. There needs to be a ritual to bring a balance to this drive for power. Presently, in the church, the only effective ritual is death.

Power can be interpreted and expressed in many different ways and for different reasons. Power itself is neither good nor bad. One may obtain the power over the flow of knowledge. Centuries ago, the church and many governments had great power in that they controlled knowledge. By controlling knowledge they controlled

---

[10] Friedrich Nietzsche, "A Nietzsche Reader", 221, 217-18: Aphorisms from Daybreak, Sections 262 and 113 (got this out of "The Soul knows No Bars" p.26)

truth, for the people were ignorant and uneducated. The people's source of knowledge was the very person or institution that controlled knowledge. This amounts to a conflict of interest. With the present technology in communications this power over knowledge is being decreased. Anyone and everyone, as displayed on the Internet, can know the truth, throughout the world. Knowledge and truth are open to everyone.

Also there is power in secrecy. **Truth knows no secrecy.** Peter [Acts 10:34; Rm 2:11] says God is impartial. Again, the Internet is bringing the truth to world, so the power of secrecy is being constricted.

An awesome power is the **power to make the rules.** Every CEO, church official, parent, knows and uses this very potent power. Rules are sometimes acceptable and necessary. But addictive power usually makes the rules so as to punish, and to keep themselves in power. When rules become a punishment they have lost their effectiveness. Even Paul [Gal 5:18] says, *"If you are led by the Spirit you are not under the law."*

One can hold on to power by the **use of force**. During the periods of the Inquisition and the Crusades, the Church used physical force to obtain and keep power. For the most part modern governments today use force as the principal means of keeping and extending power. These governments depend upon their military. US now has the mightiest military - is this good or evil?

Psychological or soul force (fear, guilt) can supply a great deal of power to individuals and organization. The Church has used and still uses this kind of force in order to retain its power.

From a spiritual and religious point of view, the only acceptable kind of power is the power of love. All religions promote love - all claim that we are to love our neighbor as we love our selves. Love should be the center of everything we do. Love is by far a greater power than anything else in the world today. Love in marriage has the ability to co-create with God another person who is made to the Image of God. There is no greater power in the world than this, and its center of power is love.

The Christian church origins were democratic and immersed in the power of love among people. Aristotle brought democracy into the world as the rule by the people. Jesus also saw the goodness of the rule by the people, for Jesus respected and trusted the people. People are created to God's Image. This is the great virtue of democracy. Regarding the power of love Jesus said, those who want to be leaders must be a servant and a slave of all (Mk 20: 25-28). Aristotle did not go this far. Jesus encouraged his disciples not to accept titles and distinctive garb or 'power clothes' which sets one above the people one serves. Jesus also stated leaders must not choose the prominent places in the assembly (Mt 23:5-11). I think Aristotle would agree.

A great decision was made in the early church about, **what to do about the gentiles.** This decision was made by the Apostles, Elders, and the whole Church of Jerusalem (Acts 15: 22), thus very democratic. Likewise in choosing a replacement for Judas, the church cast lots and thus Matthias was chosen (Acts 1:25). Leaders are to use their power as it springs out of love, and are not to obtain power from knowledge, secrecy, force or any other manner. Power was not to be used as a club, or by force, but with utmost humility and love.

The Vatican Council II made a very definite move to return the church to the rule of the people. This Council respected the great dignity and responsibility of the People of God. The Council called for shared power in the local dioceses and parish structure. In today's parish there are Parish Councils and other organizations in which lay people are to have a controlling interest. There is a great push to return to the early church practice of the people electing or choosing their servant leaders, be they bishop or pastor. The Pope is elected by Cardinals from around the world that represents the People of God. The Vatican II document on the Laity clearly states:

> *(3), The laity derive the right and duty to the apostolate from their union with Christ the head; incorporated into Christ's Mystical Body through Baptism and strengthened by the power of the Holy Spirit through Confirmation, they are assigned to the apostolate by the Lord himself. They are consecrated for the royal priesthood and the holy people (1 Pt 2:4-10).*

Trust and truth are hard to be found in a monarchical, dominating, or absolute form of governing. For generally these forms of government are defending or protecting their power. It is the duty of the laity, or the People of God, to demand a share in the government of the church. Take a look at a brief statement from the Document on the Laity No. 10:

> ***"Sharing in the function of Christ, priest, prophet and king, the laity have an active part of their own in the life and activity of the church. Their activity within the church communities is so necessary that without it the apostolate of the pastors will frequently be unable to obtain its full effect."***

It is interesting to note that Franklin D. Roosevelt said the following, "In our democracy officers of the government are the servants, and never the masters of the people." However power is a tremendous attraction and it has addictive force. We frequently hear and use that famous adage **"Power corrupts and absolute power corrupts absolutely."** This is true today. There are many examples in church, business and home life that express the addictiveness of power. And yet if power is used with humility, in the form of servant, it will be paid off with truth and trust.

The good effects of power will be that God's justice and compassion become a reality among the people. Leaders will become servants rather than masters; they will be partners rather than dominators. Jesus, who possessed absolute power, was truthful, compassionate, and just, in his dealings; he did not use power to lord it over others. He did not wear the garments of power, nor did he have the military force of power, he wasn't given to secrecy, nor did he rule by threat of punishment. He bowed to the humility of crucifixion.

John gives us another profound expression of Jesus' servanthood - he washed the feet of the disciples (Jn 13:13-15). Sr. Sandra M. Schneiders[11] indicates that John's community, of the 4th gospel, used the **"washing of the feet"** as a liturgical function. It might have been done every time they met for the liturgy. Thus Mark, Matthew, and Luke do not mention this practice, likely because their gospels were written years before John's gospel. Some scholars agree as to the importance of the foot washing. Today, sad to say, we only do the foot washing on Holy Thursday (and it is optional). I think we ought to do the 'foot washing' possibly every Sunday, for today's role of presider at the Mass has become as 'King' or 'Lord' rather than a servant wanting to **"wash the feet"** of the people.

Power is being challenged in the present day Catholic Church as it has never been challenged before. However this is based upon the fact that the church power, today, has never been more centralized in its history. So there is good reason for this type of power to be challenged. Recently Benedictine Prioress Sr. Christine Vladimiroff (Erie PA Benedictines) has checked the power of the Curia - Congregation for Institutes for Consecrated life and the Societies of Apostolic life. Sr. Christine said in part:

> **"Sr Joan Chittister, who has lived the monastic life with faith and fidelity for fifty years, must make her own decision based on her sense of church, her monastic**

---

[11] Sandra M. Schneiders, "Written That You May Believe" Herder And Herder NY, 1999, p. 108. This is a very readable and profound book on the gospel of John.

profession, and her own personal integrity. I cannot be used by the Vatican to deliver an order of silencing..."

Another Benedictine who checked the power of the Curia is, Archbishop Rembrant Weakland, O.S.B. His response to the Congregation for Worship is very prophetic as he says;

> **"I insist unequivocally that Cardinal Medina of the Cong. of Worship has not proven that I broke any liturgical norms or canons in making the decisions that were rightfully mine to make...I must defend the position that the right of the local bishop to make judgments in this diocese cannot be compromised over something as trivial as a matter of taste or opinion. I will defend my decisions... not out of stubbornness, but because, at this particular moment of history, it is my obligation to insist on the rights and duties of a local bishop in the Catholic Church."**[12]

I believe both of these incidents are very important for arresting the present power of the Curia. The Curia does not trust the Bishops of the world. Archbishop Weakland's defense of local bishops is so necessary at this time, simply because the local bishops have been brow-beaten so often in recent history that they seem to be stuck in fear of the Curia. They are certainly acting co-dependently. The Curia is the servant of the bishops not their master and governor.

The people of God have reasserted their freedom of conscience regarding birth control, and thus have checked the power

---

[12] Et cetera, "Commonweal Magazine" August 17, 2001 - Both quotes from above come from this article.

of the Vatican. There are many occasions in recent years where the 'absolute' power of the Curia is being legitimately called into question.

Power is less corruptive when it is conferred upon the leaders by the People of God. Within the church, for better than a 1000 years, the People of God conferred power upon their leaders. We cannot forget that the church is the People of God. Power of the people was certainly in the forefront in both the French and American revolutions. There are many examples in government, business, and religion where the people did not bestow power upon leaders, and great corruption resulted. Today the dictatorial, patriarchal and hierarchical systems of organizations are on the decline. One reason is that the people are more educated, and the people are demanding that their human dignity be recognized. We are created to the image of God, and people will not stand to be treated as anything less.

The Intellect makes itself secure in Patriarchy

Jesus named God Abba. Abba is the opposite of a dominating patriarch, and a great scandal to the Jews. It shows compassion, intimacy, and mutuality

Sr. Elizabeth Johnson

Even before the time of Jesus, the democratic form of government was developed in the city-state of Athens, Greece. It was a direct democracy, in which all male citizens participated in government by their vote. Socrates, Plato and Aristotle were all involved in developing this form of direct democracy. It, of course, was based on the intellect, reason and the search for truth. Women were thought not capable of reason, and they were not given the vote. Aristotle considered women as a **"*misbegotten male*"**, and it would be about two thousand years before women would be considered as being created **"*to the image of God*"**. Even St. Thomas Aquinas in the 1200s adopted Aristotle's thought regarding women. This is most difficult to understand, since the very first book of the Hebrew Bible states clearly that male and female were born equal (Gen. 1 & 2). However, the patriarchal cultures in which many religions were developed, including the Christian church, saw the church adopt a patriarchal system of government. This type of government stayed with the Catholic Church. The patriarchy made great sense in its time: it laid power at the feet of men, it was supposedly based on reason, logic and the intellect, and with absolute control there was 'peace'. Constantine used such a system in the Roman Empire: the Roman Church later adopted the same system.

It is true to say that the patriarchy as it exists in today's church is an abuse of the intellect, it is not rational, it is not just, it does not create trust, it does not produce equality, and it is not the bosom of truth. As Sr. Sandra Schneiders[13] points out so clearly;

> ***"The Institutional Church is caught in a major conundrum: how to preach a Gospel of divinely willed liberation, equality, and justice in society while maintaining***

---

[13] Sandra M. Schneiders, "Finding the Treasure", Paulist Press, NY, 2000bc, p.354

> *an institutional structure of hierarchical inequality in the Church."*

One intended effect of patriarchy is **control,** especially the control of **women**. Presently this is one great reason why patriarchy is immoral, evil and unnecessary, for women are now accepted to be **'created equal'**. We now interpret the creation stories of Genesis in that God created male and female equal, according to the 'image of God'. If this is true then patriarchy is evil, for patriarchy says by its actions that woman are not equal. This is what Aristotle believed for his time, and what was *'Ignorantia affectata'* of St. Thomas Aquinas. This ignorant belief about women keeps the patriarchy alive. Now that our culture, and hopefully the church, is getting around to accepting that women are created to the 'Image of God', room will have to be made for women in the governing circles. This spells the end of the patriarchy, and the 'old boy' network.

Fr. Diarmuid O'Murchu[14] gives a good argument for the collapse of the present patriarchy. Simply put, Jesus never envisioned a patriarchy for the Kingdom of God. In fact, everything that a patriarchy anticipates and stands for is directly opposed to Jesus' Kingdom (Greek basilicia). Jesus' Kingdom is to bring forth a radically new form of governance. Jesus is interested in people being in relationships, as is modern science - relationships based on love. The character of this relating is not based on rules or laws but on the

---

[14] Diarmuid O'Murchu, "Reclaiming Spirituality", Crossroad Pub Co., New York, 1999, p. 157-169

following: **inclusiveness** - the whole world; **equality** - no status or class, all created to God's image; **justice** - all have what they need in order to live; **liberation** - all given freedom; **peace** - harmony within the heart, home, and community; **love** - makes all things possible.

One can make a good argument that the patriarchy was Jesus' great complaint against the Temple. Jesus indicated that the temple would be destroyed; the temple needs cleansing, Jesus reluctance to pay the temple tax. All are ways in which Jesus was saying the temple has sold its heart to the patriarchy, that the temple must be destroyed.[15] The temple was the center of authority, it had power to control, power over the land, power over the money, and the power to make the rules. This might also give us some insight into the fact that the early Christians did not build magnificent basilicas or church buildings. This did not occur until Constantine (the chief patriarch) took over the church.

Another problem the institutional church has with women and patriarchy is regarding the understanding and interpretation of scripture over the centuries. The writers of scripture were not neutral, and so the text of scripture is not neutral. The ideology in which these writers wrote was patriarchal and certainly not objective. The later interpretation of these scriptures, until recent years, came out of this

---

[15] William R. Herzog II, "Jesus, Justice, Reign of God", Westminster John Knox Press, Louisville, KY, 2000, P. 111-143

same patriarchic ideology. All of this results in a very skewed and jaundice picture of women. As Sandra Schneiders[16] says:

"We get the picture of women that men created, which corresponds to the male understanding of women and their place in society at the time of the writing of these documents."

Down through the centuries the women of scripture have been demonized (Eve) and trivialized (Mary the Mother of Jesus). How difficult it is for the church just to live by the first book of the Bible, and the first chapter of the Bible, that clearly states that men and women were born equal and both shaped to the image and likeness of God. In this last century we have women as theologians, scripture scholars, canon lawyers, and moral theologians who are articulating a woman's interpretation and calling the patriarchy into question. This has never happened in the history of the church.

The Patriarchy is a great evil for Christian Asian women who come out of their culture. Mary as a virgin is interpreted not as 'biological' but as 'relational'. Indonesian theologian Marianne Katoppo indicates that Mary's virginity means she is a **"liberated human being, who - not being subject to any other human being - is free to serve God."** Virgin is **"the symbol for the autonomy of women."**[17] She is free from mans domination as it comes out of the

---

[16] Sandra M. Schneider, "Written That You May Believe", Crossroads, NY. 1999, p. 129

[17] Chung Hyun Kyung, "Struggle to be the Sun Again", Orbis Books, Maryknoll, N.Y. 1990, p. 77

Asian culture as well as the church. To quote another Korean theologian -Han Kuk Yum:

> *"The fact that in Jesus' birth, human-male is excluded connotes that a new human image, a new saving world could not longer be sustained through a patriarchal order. The human-saving Messiah who saves humanity has nothing to do with the patriarchal view of value or patriarchal order, but is totally the birth of new human image."[18]*

The virgin birth singles the end of the Patriarchy. Han thinks that if the miraculous virgin birth is important for the patriarchal church, it would be more convincing for them to insist that Jesus was born from an egg rather than a woman's body.[19] Many Asian woman theologians very bluntly state that the Patriarchy needs to be buried as it comes out of their culture as well as the Christian Church.

I have a dream that patriarchy, which is dysfunctional, will expire:

- When we realize that religious leaders are not all knowing or infallible.
- When we realize that women are needed in every stage of leadership.
- When we realize that the training married men and women receive from family responsibility is of utmost importance in church leadership.

---

[18] ibid
[19] ibid. These authors are quoted in the above book. Really a well-written and hard-hitting book concerning the theology that is developing in Asia around the Asian woman.

- When we realize that no change has occurred in the style of leadership initiated by Vatican II at the diocesan level, even though religious orders have changed.
- When we begin to train our leaders in Servant leadership style.

A new type of leadership is coming 'down the pike'. It will be more of a partnership and servant style leadership. We have waited 100s of years for this.

Truth is Disfigured by Deception

Ignorantia affectata - 'cultivated ignorance'
is an ignorance so useful that one protects it,
keeps it from the truth, in order to continue using it.
St. Thomas Aquinas

In the ancient world, the writer Diogenes reported in his famous book *"Lives of Eminent Philosophers"* that Anacharsis, a sage of the sixth century BC, defined commerce as: **"The market is a place set apart where men may deceive one another"**. I wonder if this hasn't been handed on to us. At times when the truth hurts or is not profitable, it can easily be cast aside. We often cloud truth with little **"white lies"**, or we may call it deception, misrepresentation or fraud. What ever we name it, it is a violation of truth and human dignity.

Deceit can be a very corrosive and destabilizing activity. The Enron Corporation has modeled this so well. St. Augustine said,

"Speech was given to human beings, not that we might therewith deceive one another, but that one person might make known their thoughts to another."

When we get on the slippery slop of deception, it is difficult to go back. Aristotle so wisely saw, action breeds habit, and habit can be very hard to control or break. Recall the great deception of the **"Tonkin Gulf"**, which lead us into the Vietnam War. Thousands of lives and billions of dollars were ill spent because of a deception. Psalm 34:13 says, *"Keep your tongue from evil, and your lips from speaking deceit."*

It is all very clear to us now concerning official deception (lie) that was involved in the tobacco executives declaring, under oath, that tobacco was not addictive. It is a terrible affront to the people upon learning the lying of President Clinton. Columnist Molly Mins[20] writes about the many lies that are being leveled against the people of USA by the Bush Administration; Concerning AmeriCorps, Social Security, Iraq - Weapons of Mass Destruction, global warming etc. In general people want to know the truth especially when it concerns their very life.

"All I did was tell the truth, and everyone laughed" Mark Twain

Deception can appear very tempting when a person or institution thinks that they possess absolute power. No one but God

---

[20] Molly Mins, "The Solution To Our Problems: LIE", St. Louis Post Dispatch, Editorial, Friday June 27, 2003 - Copyright Creators Syndicate

has absolute power. It is happening now within the Catholic Church when the people are told that we are not to discuss *"ordination of women"* or *"celibacy"* or other controversial topics. At times this ban on discussion is supported by *"it is God's will that we not discuss,"* most of the time it is *"we have infallible knowledge, and you are ignorant."* Intelligent people of faith know that this is a type of manipulation and deceit. The long and short of it is the people will not trust. People have the intelligence and faith to discuss such matters reasonably.

In February & March of 2002 the media has presented us with the deception and deceitful game the bishops have been playing for many years. They say, *"This is the way we have been doing it, so why change."* The media is permitting the church to get out of this deep pit it has dug for itself. The church institution is hollering and kicking for it is not used to having people outside its sheltered and walled structure telling it what it needs to do. Ellen Goodman[21] quotes from Mark Rozell of Catholic University about church and state leaders, *"History has shown, time and again, that people in public life claiming to protect the public good by secrets are protecting themselves."* They protect their agenda, their power. Paige Byrne Shortal[22] indicates that there is no need "to continue this

---

[21] Elllen Goodman St Louis Post Dispatch, "What shadows hide", Sunday March 10, 2002 p.B3
[22] Paige Byrne Shortal, St. Louis Post Dispatch, "Whose sin is it? Society?" March 12, 2002 Metro

If Aristotle Ran the Catholic Church

'secrete society' mentality". Kevin Horrigan[23] says the church has so much difficulty addressing this problem of clergy sexual abuse, that "there is a systemic problem." The deception and deceit is obvious. But I think we need to say it is also 'innocent' in the minds of the bishops, for they have always done it this way. But that innocence, to me, is what make it so necessary that there be a drastic change in the system, as Gary Wills[24] says the "Structure of deceit' must be eliminated. I find that the women and mothers have a very different outlook on this matter of clergy sexual abuse than do priests and bishops. This spells the need for a systemic change in leadership all the way to the top. If the church is a church of the truth it must include women, mothers in central leadership positions. The present leadership structure cannot reach truth without the women.

In observing deception let us look at the manner in which 'War with Iraq' is being presented to us by the administration. Many people say war is the absence of truth and the leaders who encourage war must be guilty of the lie, deceit, and deception. Lawrence LeShan[25] divides war between 'mythic reality' and 'sensory reality'. The expression of war (as presently our war with Iraq) is given to us as a myth and it is very acceptable. As a myth Chris Hedges[26] writes,

---

[23] Kevin Horrigan, St. Louis Post Dispatch, "A '50s priesthood lost—", 3/10/02 B3
[24] Gary Wills, "Papal Sin"
[25] Lawrence LeShan, 'The Psychology of War" Helios, New York, 1992. Chapter Two
[26] Chris Hedges, "War is a Force That GIves Us Meaning"Public Affairs, New YOrk, 2002, Pages 21

William L. Forst

> *"We imbue events of war with meaning they do not have... We demonize the enemy so that our opponent is no longer human* (as with Sadam Hussein and Bin Laden). *We view ourselves, our people, as the embodiment of absolute goodness."*

War cannot survive (as in Vietnam) when the press presents the reality of war. This is why in the Persian Gulf War, Afghanistan war, and now the war with Iraq, the press is restricted and under military control. The reality of war, especially our killing and slaughter, must not be aired. The truth must not be known. Wars never bring truth or justice for they function on the lie. Fear is nourished among the people (Bin Laden has been a great help in this) and this makes the lie feel like truth. With truth being absent, we instill fear, deception, and the end result is that war is good. And this is why war is complete stupidity (Using a mild ward). Simone Weil[27] who lived through the reality of World War II, writes so directly about the reality of war, *"Force is as pitiless to the man who possess it, or thinks he does, as it is to its victims; the second it crushes, the first it intoxicates."* This is one point Chris Hedges makes that war is a drug that is very addictive. We will never get control over this drug until we freely accept the 1st step of the Twelve. Admit that war is evil, that it is a drug.

Take a look at great loss of trust with the encyclical of Pope Paul VI - Humanae Vitae (1968). The Church, after 30 years, still

---

[27] Simone Weil, 'The Lliad' or 'The Poem of Force', "Wallingford, PA; Pendle Hill Pamphlet, 1993, p. 11

suffers from this deceit. Pope Paul first did not want the council fathers to discuss the matter of birth control. Some Bishops of course would take this as a mild deception. The matter of birth control had been on the mind of the People of God for 40 or more years, and it seemed like a perfect matter to discuss at the council. However, Pope John XXIII set up a special commission (1963) to discuss the matter of birth control. Before this the understanding of birth control had been set in stone with the encyclical of Pope Pius XI - Casti Connubii in 1930. The people of this new commission were to see if change was acceptable and necessary. At first the make up of the commission were celibate males. Later this was changed, and married couples were invited to take part. At first most of the theologians wanted no change from Casti Connubii. But after many months of discussion, listening to the married, and to their experiences and better understanding of the biology of it all, change would came. By the end of the commission a vast majority (52-4) of the people that made up the committee voted to change the birth control problem. During this time the commission's work was under a "gag order", which usually does not encourage trust. However, as often happens in secrecy, the commission's results leaked out. There was great rejoicing among the People of God. This commission was thought to be a wonderful result of the Vatican II council. The process was a unique experiment in open, collegial, and almost democratic discussion of an issue that was bearing down heavily upon the People of God. The commission was being very open in obtaining knowledge and information from the very people who were involved with the issue - married fathers and mothers. This might have been the first time that this was done. Can we imagine the hope and trust of the People of God? It seemed as though an incredible breakthrough in the old ways of the church was regaining the people's trust.

The Pope eventually took the minority report of the four, and a year later put out his encyclical Humanae Vitae. This of course is his right according to the Vatican rules. However, when the encyclical Humanae Vitae came out, there was a great feeling of deception, and this resulted in a deep loss of trust. Because of the high hopes that everyone had, and because of the process used to arrive at a decision, people had great trust. Even Canon Law has the Doctrine of Reception of a law. It comes out of the background of Canon 7. Church law must be based upon the good of the community. The community must have a part in the law. If the law is not good for the community it simply is not a law. Mary Kenny[28] says, *"the birth control dispute made young women (of Ireland) more hostile to the Church"*. A lack of trust that has evolved around the 'law' of birth control has had very serious consequences. In the last 30 years the leadership of the church has been bedeviled by this massive lack of trust. And the question is, when will it stop?

In the motor of human Christian relationship, trust is the oil that keeps everything moving smoothly in the right direction. When that trust is broken by lies or deception, the engine seizes up, and

---

[28] Mary Kenny, "Goodbye to Catholic Ireland", Templegate Pub. Springfield IL, 2000, p.251

movement stops. The only manner in which an organization can be run effectively is to be able to treat its people with the truth. Whether running General Motors or the Catholic Church, truth has to be the leading value of operation. When there is truth, and then there is trust. No institution needs to fear the truth. Truth may and does come from very strange places even from opposition forces. To fear it and to control it is to lose the truth as it comes from strange places. Deception or manipulation can never be used.

The respecting of truth in any organization is the responsibility of the leaders; the leaders are always to be an example. However the truth is everybody's job and responsibility. The excellence of any organization is realized when truth is shared by all people in that organization. It cannot be the sole responsibility of one person. And when all shares truth, then the organization is held together by trust.

The Intellect's Search for Truth Demands Continual Change

> "A small fluctuation may start a new revolution that will drastically change the whole behavior of the macroscopic system." Pregogin & Stengers

Our intellect certainly tells us that the only thing in life that is constant is change. It is true at all times, in all cultures, in all religions, in all business or government organizations. To stay alive we must grow and when we grow we change. On the first day that we were a blessed event in the life of our family, change began, and it does not end until death. Through life we change physically, emotionally, psychologically, spiritually and in many other ways.

The philosophers of old all indicated, many times over, that if there was to be progress, there must be change. Aristotle's idea of God as Prime Mover tickled St. Thomas' fancy, and Thomas developed his five proofs for the existence of God. Thomas brought many changes within theology with the help of Aristotle. These changes coming from a pagan philosopher was itself a great change. Astronomy pretty well accepted Aristotle's concept of the universe, until Galileo came upon the stage in the 1500s. Zoology, biology and genetics saw great changes when Darwin appeared in the middle 1800s. Newtonian physics gave way to enormous change with the coming of Einstein. In the 1900s Henry Ford developed the assembly line process for building automobiles. But the assembly line process would later see changes due to the robot and computers. In addition, unions were claiming the assembly line lowers the dignity of the human worker, and they called for change.

Within the Catholic Church there has been constant agitation for change ever since Jesus was questioned about changing some of the Jewish traditions (Mt 7:4-5). Some great changes in the early church were concerning circumcision and permitting the gentiles, women, and slaves to be Christian on an equal bases with Jews, males, and freed men. Equally remarkable changes have occurred down through the centuries; such as, the changes in doctrines of the

Church, as the Arian heresy that lasted hundreds of years, the changes within the government structure of the church - starting as a servant model in the first century, to a monarchical, patriarchal, hierarchy by the middle ages, and now back to a more collegial and servant model. Also Jesus attempted to bring about a big change in the recognition of the dignity of women.

The United States Constitution has been accredited, by many, as a work of art. It certainly has served our country well for over 200 years. We are one of the first countries of the world to adopt a written constitution. However, this constitution is not perfect, and so there is a process whereby a change can be made to the constitution. It is a difficult process to obtain change; the consent of those governed has to be obtained. The foolish, terribly bloody, senseless Civil War brought about Amendments 13, 14, & 15. The 19th in 1920 giving women the power to vote was a non-violent revolution causing fantastic changes in our society. At present, there are 23 amendments to the US Constitution. It is well to have the method of change down in print. Every law passed in the US must be in tune with the constitution.

Since the Protestant Revolution (1500s) it seems change within the church is very difficult to come by, and only appears after a horrendous struggle in the 1960s with Vatican II. This change came about in a rather haphazard manner dependent upon a particular Pope and his view of the Church. Change is not built into the system. Even today there are people in the church called 'restorationists', or those who want to restore the church to what it was before Vatican II, to a church without change. A church that cannot change is not the church of Jesus.

Possibly one reason for this inability of the church to accept and encourage change is the invention of the printing press in the 1450s. With the formation of the New Testament the 'good-news' was basically passed on by word of mouth, resulting in a glorious diversity. There is greater freedom to change with oral transformation. When the information is written down, it is objectified, it is written in stone, and the ability to change becomes very difficult. In the present, the computer and Internet, make it possible for truth to be accessible around the world instantly, in its original form, it can not be disguised. It is now difficult to control the truth, and thus to avoid change. Jesus said ***"You will know the truth, and the truth will set you free*** (Jn 8:32)." Despite all of this some leaders of the present Catholic Church still believe that they can control what is the 'truth', and thus there is no need for change.

The Catholic Church at the present time is facing many profound changes - globalization, inculteration, and the place of women, the authority structure, ecumenism, and the use of power. The Catholic Church doesn't have a legally accepted or orderly manner to bring about change, as does the US Constitution. The manner in which changes occur depends upon the person who is pope at any given time. What are needed are the 'checks and balances', and an 'opposition party' which is written into the US constitution. This helps change to be an ongoing affair.

As for change, let us take a very short look at Vatican II Council, called by Pope John XXIII, 1962-1965. From the beginning of the council the Curia (Pope's cabinet) was opposed to change. Quickly it became clear that the Curia in preparing the agenda would bring no changes what so ever. It was obvious that the Curia's power would have to be restrained. Pope John was in favor of this. By 1965 the 2000 bishops representing the world brought many radical and needed changes to the church. This was democracy at its best.

Two dominant changes coming out of Vatican II are contained in two words presently hardly used: **collegiality** (decisions made by many) and **subsidiarity** (trust that the people of God can do it). These two ideas respect the dignity of the human being created to God's Image, and the idea that the Spirit of God is given to all. But before the collegiality and subsidiarity are put into practice, the dominating patriarchal system, built up over hundreds of years, will have to be dismantled. This may be a greatest change the church has seen since the admittance of the gentiles in the first years of the church. There is great hope that the People o God will bring these needed changes.

The primary drive of the **patriarchy** is the domination of women by men. This has worked its way into every aspect of the world's culture and society. Women seem to be the main focus, but patriarchy weaves its dominating features into class, race, sexual orientation, age, wealth, ordained, and titles of power as well. Patriarchy infects every aspect of church and state. There is a terrible struggle going on presently to free people from this evil.

Let us consider one change, from Vatican II Council, that of Religious Freedom. For many years the Vatican looked upon the American Catholic church as suspect with its policy of separation of church and state, religious freedom, and freedom of the press. Pope Gregory XVI gave his encyclical *"Mirari vos"* in 1832 in which he condemned liberty of conscience, freedom of the press, and separation of church and state. The many Popes after Gregory continued this stand. At Vatican II, after a great deal of vigorous discussion, and the guidance of Cardinal Spellman and Fr. John Courtney Murray S.J., religious freedom and freedom of conscious was accepted. This was a very radical but needed change for the Church to make.

For two hundred years, there has been a group of prominent churchmen who have advocated that a written Constitution be adopted for the Universal or Catholic Church, as well as for the thousands of dioceses and parishes within the church. Today Leonard Swidler is a leader in this regard.[29] A **written constitution** lays open the rights and responsibilities of the various people involved in the Church e.g. Pope, Bishops, Pastors and Lay people. It provides for a uniform and just manner of succession. A written constitution provides for a deliberate and wise method of change. Finally, a constitution is the joint work of the people being governed, which is the Body of Christ.

---

[29] Swidler, Leonard, "Toward a Catholic Constitution", (Crossroad Pub Co. N.Y.) 1996. Leonard gives a look at Vatican II's turn to freedom and dialogue. Also he gives a great history of a written constitution within the American Church. His work is very well researched.

The first Bishop of the United States - Bishop John Carroll of Baltimore (1789), was elected by the priests of the nation - a democratic process. This practice continued for a number of years. Bishop John England of Charleston SC (1820), called a constitutional convention in his diocese (states of SC, NC, & GA), and with the People of God developed a written constitution that governed the diocese until Archbishop England's death in 1842. Bishop England was the first Bishop to address U.S. Congress in 1826. He extolled the U.S. Constitution and indicated that Congress need not fear Rome, for the Catholic Church welcomes this form of government.

I want to close this part of our discussion by giving you a quote from Fr. Teilhard de Chardin. The essay is **"Mastery of the World and the Kingdom of God**," written in 1916. Chardin was involved World War I as a soldier (not a chaplain), he served on the front lines in many battles in France, for a period of four years. I believe his observations in the midst of all of this are very prophetic:

> *"Never again, please God, may we be able to say of religion that its influence has made people more indolent, more unenterprising, less human; never again may its attitude lie open to the damming suspicion that it seeks to replace science by theology, effort by prayer, battle by resignation, and that its dogmas may well debase the value of the world by limiting in advance the scope of inquiry and the sphere of energy. Never again, I pray, may anyone dare to complain of Rome that it is afraid of anything that moves and thinks".*[30]

---

[30] Ursula King, "Spirit of Fire", (Orbis Books, New York, 10545, 1998) p. 59-64

William L. Forst

From Truth Equality most follow

What is a friend? A single soul dwelling in two bodies
Aristotle

Aristotle believed that all those living in a *polis* (city) should be equal citizens (his weakness was that he did not include women, and slaves) able to participate in government. The citizens have equal rights, speech and power. The place where these free citizens met to deliberate and decide the welfare of their *polis* was called - *ekklesia* (our word for church). The real meaning of *ekklesia* is best rendered **"public assembly of the political community"** or **"democratic assembly of full citizens,"**[31] the early Christians adopted this word and idea for its church. One great problem, and probably a cause for persecutions in the early church, was that early Church was too democratic, it included all baptized in their **Ekklesia** - men and women, slave and free, gentile and Jew. Not just **"free men,"** but everyone was part of the democratic assembly. This was very revolutionary. The modern Catholic Church needs to be more aware of our democratic beginnings.

The Declaration of Independence, in 1776, was approved by all the delegates from the 13 colonies. In part it reads:

---

[31] Eugene C. Bianchi, "A democratic Catholic Church", (Crossroad, New York, 1992) P.19

"We hold these truths to be self-evident, that all men are created equal, that they are endowed by their Creator with certain unalienable Rights, that among these are Life, Liberty, and the pursuit of Happiness. That to secure these rights, Governments are instituted among Men, deriving their just powers from the consent of the governed".

We all know how imperfect this document is and how it has taken a terrible war (Civil), and 200 years of hard work to be successful in understanding its true meaning. We are still not quite there. The intent of the framers is that they wanted no more oppression from a very patriarchal and dominant system. They wanted equality. They wanted freedom. They wanted a drastic change, and they had no idea what this would mean. Many of the ideals the colonists were playing with came out of the scriptures—human beings are created to God's image, they have intelligence and free will, they wanted to live in a government that is formed by all the people, not a government imposed upon them. The United States would be ruled by the whole people and not by individuals, such as kings, dictators, or monarchs. The leaders in a democracy are to be servants of the people.

The modern day church is looking this change straight in the face - that all people in the church are created equal, and that we are created to God's Image. This reminds us of Paul's concern about baptism - is everyone equal in God's eyes, or are some less equal than others? Paul answers this problem [Gal 3:27-28]

William L. Forst

> *"As many of you as were baptized into Christ have clothed yourselves with Christ. There is no longer Jew or Greek, there is no longer slave or free, there is no longer male and female; for all of you are one in Christ Jesus."*

The modern church has been attempting to better itself by looking at its parts - the priests, sisters, diocese, lay people, bishops and pope. Renewal must come from the whole. The parts are not the whole, and the Pope is not the Church. But by examining the parts it can lead to a renewed whole. Margaret Wheatley[32] states, **"We need to work with the whole of the system, even as we work with individual parts or isolated problems."** We can understand the whole by trying to understand how the whole is influencing or affecting the local level or parts. The whole is not the Vatican, or the Curia, or the Pope. The whole is the Body of Christ, the Church, and the People of God. This is very difficult for the western mind to get into its thinking. This is the reason we have, for so many years, considered the whole as the person at the top, or the CEO of General Motors, or the pope. The parts were described as a small piece, a replica, of the whole.

The eastern mind, or the Buddhist, sees this problem very differently. Thich Nhat Hanh[33] says:

> *All things depend on all other things for their existence. Take, for example, this leaf...earth, water, sea,*

---

[32] ibid Wheatley - p. 137-140
[33] Thich Nhat Hanh, "Old Path White Clouds: Walking in the Footsteps of the Buddha" Berkeley, CA 1991 . p.169

tree, clouds, sun, time, space—all these elements have enabled this leaf to come into existence. If just one of these elements was missing, the leaf could not exist. All beings rely on the law of dependent co-arising. The source of one thing is all things".

This is what Jesus designed. The church is the People of God. The people of God form the whole. The people of God are equal, the people include everyone, and there are no distinctions. The people of God make up the whole. We understand the parts - parish, diocese, layperson, priest, sister, brother, monsignor, bishop, pope - by understanding the whole and how the whole relates to the parts.

For instance, between 1965-1975 the US Catholic Church lost 60,000 middle management people (brother, sisters, priest and bishops). The institution (not the People of God) looked upon this exodus as a loss; it was their fault, they chose not to live up to their promises, we will do without them. It is saying that the 60,000 are sinful people. But the church never really has examined the relationship between the institution and these middle management people. How was this relationship affected? How has the whole been affected? What happened in the whole that caused this effect? How could the whole change in order to reconcile this loss? What happened in the institution to bring on this exodus? How can this be corrected?

It is important to learn from mistakes made either by the institution or by the people. It is necessary for the institution to deal with diversity, difference of opinion, and mistakes. It should not look upon these matters with fear or denial. Out of this difference and diversity will come meaning and truth. The meaning will come from the People of God, from the meaning will come change, and change will be looked upon as a friend, for it will be a source of new life.

The Church is forever doing a balancing act.

Chapter # 2

Aesthetics is directed toward Beauty – p. 45
Creativity-Imagination is the bedrock of Aesthetics – p. 50
Aesthetics is Beauty through Networking – p. 57
The Feminine is at the Heart of Aesthetics – p. 62
Aesthetics as Diversity, Diversity as Beauty – p. 70

Aesthetics is directed toward Beauty

"All beauty yearns to be conspicuous". You taste grace,
you want to make it known. Thomas Aquinas

"The proper use of the imagination is to give beauty to the world." Lin Yutang

There are four transcendentals, **Truth - Beauty - Goodness - Unity**. We call them transcendentals because they rise-above/go beyond everything in the world. The Greek philosopher Plato developed the philosophical concept of transcendence. He affirmed the existence of absolute goodness, which he characterized as something beyond description and as knowable ultimately only through intuition. Aesthetics is directed toward Beauty.

Aesthetic is a pretty fancy word, which is difficult to pronounce, and not used frequently. But the word comes from Greek and has a clear meaning *"sense of perception"*. It is aesthetics that draw us to beauty. Beauty can be seen in all manner of animate and inanimate life. Beauty may be observed in works of the human mind, such as painting, construction, architecture, homily, philosophy, theology etc. The human being is normally inspired by beauty, but not all beauty enlivens every human being. The beauty of the human beings is their diversity, and the diversity of beauty that human beings are capable of producing. Peace and contentment can be the result of beauty. The greatest beauty of the human being is that we are made to the image of God.

In our modern culture, I think it is difficult for us to detect beauty or *"to smell the roses"*. Many of us seemed to be so attracted by the consumerism of our time, that we only want to *"sell the roses"*. Frequently our work does not allow us the time to admire or create beauty. But it is very important for us, especially as leaders, to make time in order to observe the beauty around us. I, as a catholic priest, am asked to make a retreat each year. This is really a time of observing beauty as it appears in one's life. Frequently I have made this retreat at Assumption Trappist monastery in Ava, Missouri. The place includes 3800 acres of the Missouri Ozarks. There are long rugged walks along fresh water creeks and up a mountain to sit in a deer stand gazing over miles of hills decorated with beauty. The setting to me is all about beauty and truth, and it certainly helps me to imagine the beauty God gave me as his image. Possibly this is one reason why many retreat centers for business, educational and church people are in places of great environmental beauty. Certainly the government & church must do more to protect the aesthetics of God's environment.

For one's work or job to be meaningful we must find beauty in it. In reading the book "Fast Food Nation" by Eric Schlosser[34], the manner in which management treats their minimum waged workers does not generate beauty. Management demands blind obedience from the workers. They determine exactly how a task is to be performed. Management imposes its rules about pace, output, quality, and technique. There is no room for creativity. Management does not depend upon the skills or talents of the workers, but this is built into the operating systems and machines. This makes the workers interchangeable and cheap, and no doubt the reason for the 80% to 90% turn over of workers. There is very little in the job to attract them, there is no beauty.

Some people, who possibly do not find beauty on the job, create it in and around their home or their 'place'. I do think it is in everyone's genes to create beauty, and to be inspired by the beauty they see around them. I have two nieces who are executives in large corporations, and yet they find time to create beautiful gardens around their homes. When I first saw the home of my niece living in Connecticut, I said, *"Mary Beth, who does the gardening?"* Thinking she certainly does not have the time to work this garden. She said, *"I do"*. Not satisfied with this, I said, *"Do you get any help?"* She said, *"No. I find gardening very relaxing, and it gives me ways to be creative. I find it is an expression of beauty"*. I thought to myself her yard is like a symphony. There are many different flowers,

---

[34] Eric Schlosser, "Fast Food Nation", Houghton Mifflin Co. New York, 2001 p.73-

shrubs, and plants as an orchestra uses many different instruments. There is a great deal of practice (cultivation), and creativity involved in both symphony and garden. She ultimately is expressing the beauty of God, of whose image she is. She is a much better leader stemming from the fact that she has created this beauty around her. She will more easily be able to see the beauty in others.

Beauty is uplifting and beauty liberates, but the lack of it can depress and imprison a person. Consider the Vatican Museum, the Sistine chapel; the St. Louis Arch. How exhilarating it can be for the people to view the works of Michelangelo, Bramante or Raphael, and Eero Saarinen. The spirit of many people have been freed and lifted by viewing their work. On the other hand, consider the drab and ugly look of many of our inner cities or our prisons. The folks living in the inner city feel as though they are in a prison, they become depressed and prone to anger and violence. This should not be permitted to happen. Why does the Catholic Church pull out of the inner city? The Church has much beauty to offer these city dwellers, who are usually the poor.

To me, the severe decline in priests (Catholic Church) is a lack of aesthetics or beauty in observing the composition of the priesthood. In the last couple of decades there has been great control demanded of the priesthood, and upon the priest. The control demanded is to keep the old order. This makes the prophetic impossible to express. The church seems to be controlling the manner in which priests and people contact the Spirit of God. The result is to block the aesthetic and beauty of God. Cardinal Danneels suggest that the experience of beauty within theology, morals and liturgy is vitally important. He says:

> *"Beauty can make a synthesis of the true and the good. Truth, Goodness, Beauty. Here are three names and three access roads to God. But Beauty has been explored very little in theology and catechesis in our day. Is it not time to attend to this lacuna?"*[35]

Science has a beautiful manner in their approach to aesthetics and beauty. Kuhnts calls it **"Resolution of Revolution".**[36] First they accept that scientific theories are not infallible, nor are the solutions achieved ever perfect. The fallibility of a scientific theory will inevitably generate a crisis. The crises occurs when the accepted theory is disproved or seriously questioned. A theory that may have been held supreme for 100s of years is now questioned. This spells chaos. Two or more groups are thrust together defending the 'truth' of the old theory against the upstarts. The institution that upholds the theory begins to arrange the wagons in a circle to defend.

A huge difficulty here is that most institutions - be they religious, government, business, or education have their bureaucracies that do not welcome change. They almost always choose the status quo. On the other hand, the fallibility of theology, the fallibility of business and educational theory has a built in ability to generate a crises. As the theologian Ivone Gebrara has said, ***"When you invite***

---

[35] America Magazine, 30 July - August 6 2001, p. 9
[36] Kuhnts, "Structure of Scientific Revolution", Phoenix Books, University of Chicago, 1962

people to think you are inviting revolution". In the Catholic Church the dogma of infallibility is wiping out aesthetics, imagination, and creativity. Even Paul states clearly (Thess 5:19) ***"Do not stifle the Spirit, do not despise prophecies, test everything: retain what is good."*** If the aesthetics of the priesthood, of ecumenism, etc. are to be explored then the church will have to welcome crises and chaos within its system. It cannot continue to stifle the Spirit of God. Servant leaders will see to it that beauty is present and obtainable with the people they lead.

Creativity-Imagination is the bedrock of Aesthetics

> "The zest for life, which is the source of all passion
> and all insight, even divine,
> does not come to us from ourselves...
> It is God who has to give us the impulse of wanting him."
> **Teilhard de Chardin**

I built a sculpture, standing in a field; its name is *'pneuma'*. See pneuma at the end of this chapter. In Greek pneuma means breath, wind, soul, and it is the church's word for Spirit, the Spirit of God. My pneuma is made of farm implement junk that I obtained from my friends **Sylvan and Joan Nichting** of Pilot Grove, IA. They run a Case-International Farm Implement Co. Pneuma weighs more than a ½ ton. The top is about twelve feet into the heavens. The main center pole is a 10 ft. axel off an old combine. It has four spinners, two are small, but one is large with four steel disks, which weighs more than 150 pounds. Pneuma has a large tail to catch the wind. The amazing thing about this large, bulky, ugly, heavy structure is that it moves with the wind with gentle ease. Sometimes the wind blows pneuma to the north, other times to the southwest. Pneuma does not move the wind but the wind moves it, even though it weighs ½ ton. The bulky, global, 2000 years old Catholic Church should also be moved by the Spirit, and not the church moving the Spirit. For the Church to respond to the Spirit it has to be always ready to change (sometimes to the north, then to the south) and, at times, change in ways it has not imagined. The Church institution (Pope & Curia) is not in the drivers seat. The institution is the bulky, ugly, very large and heavy structure that is to be moved by the Spirit of God. When the church institution has leaders who cannot recognize aesthetics, they will not welcome change. These leaders demand control; for it is in control that their power is felt. They will not let the Spirit move them, but they attempt to move the Spirit.

Pneuma gives us a beautiful and expressive facsimile of the Spirit of God working in each of us and in the institution. As Jesus says,

> **"The wind blows where it wills, and you can hear the sound it makes, but you do not know where it comes from or where it goes; so it is with everyone who is born of the Spirit [Jn 3:8]."**

This was very confusing to Nicodemus, to the early Church, and even to the Church of our times. The reason for concern here is that Spirit does not bend to church law, business principles, or the power people of human organizations. The Spirit of God moves where it wills. The Spirit of God connects with the intellect, creativity, and imagination (all gifts of God) of the People of God. With this mixture of Spirit + intellect + imagination + creativity = new creation. This is true in any institution that permits the Spirit to work freely.

Just imagine what was brought about by the creative spirit of Nickolaus August Otto (1832-91) and the gasoline engine, and Rudolf Christian Diesel in creating the diesel engine. Where would the world be without the creative imagination of **Benjamin Franklin** (1706-1790) who invented bifocal spectacles, lightening rods, or his experiments in electricity (1846), or the famous kite experiment (1852)? Also all that Franklin did was joined with Luigi Galvini and Alessandro Volta to give us electric batteries. Christian Oersted, Faraday, James Joule etc. built on their creativeness to bring us the electric power that we are so dependent upon today. We continue to grapple with the many changes that have come to our culture because of the Quantum theory of physics. All of this comes from the Spirit of God, the pneuma.

The pneuma, the **Spirit of God**, has been lavishly active in all Churches - Buddhist, Islamic, Christian etc. Where would the Christian church be if Paul were not able to use his creative imagination in reference to being the ***"Apostle to the Gentiles?*** [Rom 11:13]" Paul did this in face of great opposition from the Church institution, however the Spirit of God gave him strength. Francis of

Assisi bringing the church in line with the *"cry of the poor"*. He too was rebuked for disturbing *"good order"* within the Church. St. **Thomas Aquinas** who, against objection, brought in Aristotle's thinking to theology. Not to mention the millions of couples around the world who are using their creative-imagination connected with the Spirit in determining their bedroom activity. They no doubt think that the Church needs to trust the married couples in making Spirit filled decisions about their inner life.

Creativity and imagination is the very heart of all religions, it is the manner in which we meet the Spirit of God. With creativity and imagination we come to the realization of who we are, what are the talents and gifts God has given us To create an image in one's mind, to create an image on the paper, to create an idea, is very god-like. It is in creating that we realize that we are God's Image. To create a character, to make her face sad or joyful, to give this person revolutionary ideas, is to create a new world. To create is to bring in new life - a rebirth, a death to the old and resurrection to the new.

The many parables, or stories, of Jesus 'tease the mind' and excite the imagination. Sometimes the parable startles the imagination e.g. the Samaritan Woman at the well, or the Prodigal Son. The parables give rise to a new way of thinking or new style of acting. Jesus' parables can only spell change in our life when they are received in freedom. Men and women interpret Jesus' parables differently, our neighbor interprets differently, and certainly people of different cultures understand differently. This because we all develop different imaginations.

William L. Forst

The effectiveness of the many beautiful liturgical rituals of the Christian church is based upon aesthetics. Aesthetics helps to make the ritual active rather than **'obligation'** or passive. How often do good catholic people do the sacraments out of obligation (Mass), which spells pure drudgery? It is always the same. It is pure obligation. Many of us memorized the Baltimore Catechism - to what avail. When love is arrived at from 'obligation' it dispels the heart. How easy it is to repeat from memory, to repeat mindlessly, the rituals of the church. These same rituals when done aesthetically will move the heart to love, and this can move God to do the impossible.

Washington Post[37] remarks about the amazing developments in the **scientific imagination**. There are a great number of radical scientific developments in the last century, there are many to come in the years ahead. As many as 90% of all scientist who have ever lived are alive today. I suspect we could say that of theologians and scripture scholars that 90% of all theologians who have ever lived are alive today. Imagine the amazing theological developments that are available to us today?

In the past four decades, we have created more scientific knowledge than in the previous 5,000 years. I am sure this may be true with theology and scripture study. The reason that science has amassed this amount of information is the **First Law of High Tech**: It happens with the free use of intelligence, imagination and creativity. The scientists are *'thinking outside the box.'* The church has much to

---

[37] Joel Garreau, "Washington Post National Weekly" August 20-26, 2001, p.10

learn about the scientific axiom. It is generally outside the box that we respond to the Spirit of God.

An organization expresses trust in their members when the worker's imagination and creativity are given the freedom to function. An institution that shows this trust will receive trust in return. Every human organization, especially the Church, needs the creative-imagination of its members. This was the fire and intensity of the early church. It was the fire and intensity for 15 years after Vatican II. I have a friend, Mary Lea Reuter, who teaches 4th grade in the Tucson AZ public school, located in the desert. In 2001 she told me that the teachers organized an **"Out of Box"** committee with the consent of the principal. All teachers are invited, but not all participate. The teachers want to express their imagination without any restrictions. All ideas accepted as they are put through free dialogue of the group. No idea gets marked 'unacceptable". It is in this manner that the teachers get in touch with the aesthetics of teaching; they freely can use their creativity and imagination. New ideas emerge and better teaching.

Mr. Jerry Brewer[38] of Brewer Science (BCI), Rolla, MO **"Broke out of the box".** Jerry worked for big corporations of Texas Instruments and Honeywell. He said of his work;

> *"They have this little square container that is already contracted and you're just stuffed in it. So, as a person, your ability to grow your own abilities and strengths stops."*

---

[38] Rachel Melcher, St. Louis Post, Section 3, Pages 1 & 5, Monday May 5, 2003

Jerry started his own company on a wing and mostly a prayer. He wanted to encourage creativity of the workers, and to empower the individual. Since 1980 BSI has grown into a rather large 'small' business. Samuel Fromartz,[39] headlines, **"Command-and control managers strangle creativity."** Today all of the above is true in Church business - creativity is strangled by the 'command-and control' style of leadership. The Spirit of God is being controlled.

When an organization suppresses the creativity of it's members, or eliminates the possibility of making a mistake, we eliminate the Spirit of God. This is what the Church did with **Martin Luther** (and many modern day theologians), they considered him a mistake and sinner, and did not consider him an opportunity. The Church could not bring itself to consider Luther's creativity. Luther was **'*Thinking Outside the Box'*.** The Church was interested in status quo, and lost a tremendous opportunity.

Music is a beautiful expression of one's creativity and imagination. The Mass with proper music can bring the fire of the Spirit on those present. I write more at length about the importance of aesthetics as expressed by music in the **conclusion**.

Fr. Roger Haight[40] writes about imagination:

> *Using Aristotelian and Thomistic categories, the imagination is one of four inner senses that always accompanies human knowing, because all knowledge is*

---
[39] Samuel Fromartz, St. Louis Post, Section C5, Monday May 5, 2003
[40] Roger Haight, "Jesus Symbol of God", Orbis Press, NY 2000 p. 37-39

drawn out of the data of the external senses and mediated to understanding through, among other things, concrete images that are in turn stored in the memory."

When the creativity and imagination of the members are accepted we have life, we have movement, we have change, we are responding to God's Spirit. We need not fear. We have what Jesus said, **"I have come to light a fire on earth** [Lk 12:49]." This is the heart of aesthetics

Aesthetics is Beauty through Networking

"Collaboration is the real energy of human striving and accomplishment, not competition." Bishop Sims

In one sense networking is a word that is new and springs from modern computing. But actually it is as old as the human race, at least the human race described as existing in the Paleolithic age - about 12,000 BC. Riane Eisler[41] describes the people of the Paleolithic age as worshipping a female God or Goddess - God the Mother, rather than God the Father. This is so because of a woman's fantastic gift of co-creating with God in bringing forth-new life. The female Goddess networked with all humans and lived in peace. There is no indication that there were wars, no domination, and no private possession of land. These societies networked. It is a great beauty.

---

[41] Riane Eisler, "The Chalice & the Blade", Harper San Francisco, CA.1988

William L. Forst

The patriarchy seems to begin with the age of agriculture, about 10,000 BC. The male was strong, took possession of land, made wars to get more land, enslaved people, and there was little or no networking, nor was there peace.

Aristotle, 300 BC, would advocate a type of networking in a democratic system - rule by the people. He understood the great defects of a patriarchy. However his system was fallible and has endured many changes up to our day.

Jesus built upon Aristotle's ideas and called the people of God to network out of love. Jesus would advocate networking when he said all law and the prophets are involved in this one statement, *"love your neighbor as yourself".* The first council of Jerusalem [Acts 15:22] included apostles, presbyters and the whole infant church. This council was brought together in a networking fashion, for it could only work when centered in love. The council decided that baptism makes gentiles, women, and slaves equal members of the Christian church. God shows no partiality, all people are created equal.

This networking would continue until **Constantine** took over the Church in the 300sAD. The church and state became one, with the state being the principal power. A few hundred years later this was turned around in that the church was the principal power over the state. This system exists in some countries today. Constantine's Roman system of government was based on a hierarchy and caste system. The Roman Catholic Church bought into this system hook-line-and-sinker. Out of this we got **the patriarchy**, the rule by men.

Now the People of God would not be trusted, the people are not treated as God's image. Women, once again, were put in their place, and considered **"misbegotten males."**

To a computer addict Networking means the following: enabling others, trusting others research and conclusions, it means flexible organization, it means emphasizing creativity and imagination, accepting change as new life, finally it means cooperation. This **networking** is all about relationship, how one computer relates to another computer. In church terms it means relating to our neighbor in love. In human organizations networking can only be accomplished with love. The traditional system of organization that many corporations follow, and probably all church institutions, is not networking. The traditional system the church presently depends upon relies on a centrally controlling, dominating, dictatorial type of organization. All power comes from and is centered upon the top, usually a top man (King, CEO, Pastor, Pope). To hold this together a hierarchical caste system is developed. The employees are kept in line by fear, coercion, manipulation and sometimes by force. The employees are functionaries; they are not trusted. The employee's creativity and imagination is suspect. Whistle blowers are put out. This kind of organization resists change at any price. Finally there is very little cooperation among the members of the institution. The top man says **'the buck stops here'** for he alone is responsible, he has all the power. Networking is seen as cumbersome, slow and unnecessary. In a Christian sense there is little relationship, little love, and the main motive is *'do what you are told to do, don't ask questions.'*

What would happen to the Catholic Church if it were organized around networking rather than around a top down power and caste system? Simply put the institution would have to implement two concepts that come out of Vatican Council II (1962-65). The one concept is **"Collegiality"**. This simply means a collection of people who make decisions by listening to and trusting one another. In particular it means that the power of the institution rests firmly on the shoulders of the Bishops of the world in full union with the Bishop of Rome. The Bishops are servants of the People of God, not their lord and masters. In this manner collegiality would involve the **"People of God"** who are considered the Church. People must be trusted, the People are God's Image, and the People of God have equal access to the Spirit of God. Networking would build a system whereby all the people would be trusted and involved in the operation of the institution called the Catholic Church. It would mean that power would be diffused. It would also convey that the patriarchy is defunct.

Networking would use another concept of the Vatican Council II '**Subsidiarity**'. This concept makes a centralizing power control of an organization impossible. It means simply that what can be done at a lower level must be done there. What the Republicans are always calling for but never quite accomplish - take power from the federal government and give it to the states. The present system existing in the church today is extremely central power conscious. The central power has to make all the decisions. This is also called micromanaging. This type of management will not trust the people below, the **'People of God'**. In the Church subsidiarity would mean that the local Bishops, the local Pastors, and ultimately the **'People of God'** would be trusted. The Curia would once again become a functionary of the Pope; it would pass messages from the Pope to the global church. The Curia would not legislate; it would not make decisions for the local Bishops. The church institution would promote relationships within parishes, dioceses, and the global church. It would not demand how the relationship would work; it would stop using fear (excommunication) to perform its duties. It would learn how to forgive and how to love. Obviously this would bring about a Copernican revolution within the Church. In fact, it would bring a new life, a sharing in the death (to the old system) and resurrection (new life) of Jesus.

It might be well to quote from the new science as to how networking works with quarks, particles, and waves. This taken from Lipnick & Stamps.[42]

> *"Networks work because of the dynamic relationships that transpire among the people involved. To understand the process of networking, we have to shift from thinking about things and the way they are built, to thinking about relationships and the way they behave."*

---

[42] Lipnack, J. & Stamps, J. "The Networking Book", Routledge and Kegan Paul. 1986

William L. Forst

The Feminine is at the Heart of Aesthetics

"Woman does not possess the image of God in herself, but only when taken together with the male who is her head, so that the whole substance is one image."
Augustine

How far we have grown from Augustine? Women are very much a part of aesthetics and beauty of the world. They have suffered immeasurably through the centuries. The Christian Church has such an enlightened devotion and reverence for the Mother of Jesus. The Church has been dealing with the proper devotion to Mary for 2000 years. Jesus has commanded the Church to respect women as being the Image of God. In this century respect for Mary and women has been on an upward thrust.

We must refer once again to the teachings of Aristotle about women. He said that full excellence could be realized only by the mature male adult of the upper class, not by women, or children. He referred to women as ***"misbegotten males"***. Aristotle and Plato both thought that women were not capable of reason and logic, and therefore should not be educated and certainly would not be given the right to vote. Women were considered chattel. The Catholic Church through history has revised somewhat this view of women.

Jesus set the standard for realizing the dignity and respect for women. Jesus broke many of his church customs and traditions in order to express his respect for women. Again today we will have to

If Aristotle Ran the Catholic Church

break some church traditions in order to arrive at a greater dignity for women. In John's gospel (4:3-42) we need to look at the story of the **"Women at the Well"**. She was some kind of recovering addict, but she knew the scriptures and discussed theology with Jesus in public, and then made a proclamation to her people. All of this was encouraged and approved of by Jesus, but also was a violation of Jewish church rules and traditions. Jesus was showing his church how they were missing the boat in aesthetics. Sandra M. Schneiders[43] in writing about the 4th gospel presents women positively and as having intimate relation with Jesus. So much so that Schneiders says:

> *"Whoever the author of the Fourth Gospel was, it was someone who had a remarkable rich and nuanced understanding of feminine religious experience… If women Christians in Johns' community had been restricted to the domestic and religious roles of women in the Jewish world of that period, it is very difficult to imagine where the evangelist got such extraordinarily rich insights into the relationship of women with Jesus."*[44]

The granting of leadership roles to women was certainly not the practice, in church or state, for Jesus' time. But the early Christian Church attempted to treat women as God's Image and equal with their male partners. The roll of women was established, as is indicated in the gospels of John & Mark, when Jesus meets Mary

---

[43] Sandra M. Schneiders, "Written That You May Believe", Crossroads Pub, NY, 1999, p. 98-113. A great book that brings out many new and different ideas from a woman's view..
[44] Ibid p. 99

Magdalyn at the resurrection. Mary then announced to the other disciples *"**She has seen the Lord. (20:18)**"* This amazing event gives us a forceful view of the roll of women in the Christian Community. Sandra Schneiders[45] a scripture scholar gives her view of this;

> *John's resurrection shows us that a woman was regarded as the primary witness to the paschal mystery... Her claim to apostleship is equal in every respect to both Peter and Paul's... Unlike Peter, she was not unfaithful to Jesus during the passion, and unlike Paul, she never persecuted Christ in his members. But, like both, she saw the risen Lord, received directly from him the commission to preach the Gospel, and carried out that commission faithfully and effectively."*

Jesus was simply being a prophet and said, ***"Thus Says the Lord,"*** women are *'**God's Image**'* and must be treated with the respect God has bestowed upon them.

The practice of Baptism as an entrance rite was a radical change from Jewish practice. **Male - female, slave - free, gentile - Jew were all baptized as equals.** We know Phoebe was a deaconess (Rom 16:1), along with other deaconesses. There was a husband & wife team - Prisca and Aquila - who had Church in their home (Rom 16: 3-5). Finally there were some women, along with men, who headed ***"house churches."***

With the Edict of Milan (313BC), much of church practice regarding women as equals was canceled. Constantine recognized the Church as a legal entity and then proceeded to take over the Church.

---

[45] Ibid p. 113

This period was called *"Caesaro-Papism"* or Caesar is Pope. This was a good time for the Church, in that the persecutions were stopped, and the church had a certain amount of freedom. But it was an injurious time, in that the Church was dominated by a secular powers, servant leadership was out. This situation lasted for hundreds of years. It was during this time that the Christian church adopted the monarchical type of government. The Bishops would become little (sometimes big), secular princes. There now was a great distinction between lay and clergy, between men and women. Women would pay the bill by losing much of what they had gained.

By the 1200s St. Thomas Aquinas appears on the scene. It was Thomas who introduced the Church to the secular Greek philosophers, especially Aristotle. He built a theological system that was called *"Scholasticism"*. Thomas did almost nothing to change Aristotle's ignorant views of women. Scholasticism produced a great deal that was good and excellent for the growth of the Church. However in his Summa (Suppl. q.39a 1) Thomas maintains that **"because women are in a state of subordination"** they cannot receive ordination or any church office. The birth of a woman is a defect of nature; she is a *"misbegotten man"*. And the fault was caused by the conjugal act. The conjugal act was considered sinful by Augustine (400sAD). The Roman Catechism that came out of the Council of Trent -1566 p.247 said;

"Believers are to be taught not to have relations for the sake of lust or sensual desire, but within the boundaries prescribed by the Lord. For it is becoming to recall the

warning of the Apostle: 'Let those who have wives live as though they had none', and further remember the saying of St. Jerome: ***'The wise man should love his wife with reason and not with passion...".***

Know well that the leaders of the Church were probably in good conscience during this time, but they were also, it seems, in deep ignorance. The position Thomas took on women, both mentally and spiritually was far from the position of Jesus.

It is interesting to note what was happening with women in the 1600s-1700s in Europe. Olwen Hufton[46] helps us to understand that women in general were freed, and their dignity was better accepted coming from the example of the **religious orders** of women in those days. Women were always under the control of a father or husband, and in religious orders women were kept in cloister or enclosure, also under the control of a Bishop or Priest. A few years after Pope Urban VIII in 1629 issued an order that the **Ursulines** of Paris were to live in strict enclosure, came a rich widow **Louise de Marillac**. Louise together with her spiritual director, Vincent de Paul, began to realize that women have to have access to the streets in order to take care of the poor, the sick, and to teach the children. Eventually these two would receive permission from Pope Urban to do just that. Within 100 years there were many religious orders of women (Sisters of Charity, St. Joseph, Notre Dame etc.) and thousands of women doing works of Christian charity outside the *"clasura"* doing the real work

---

[46] Olwen Hufton; "The Prospect Before Her", (Alfred A. Knope, N.Y.) 1996 p. 363-400.

of the church. Most of these orders adopted a uniform of dress that was similar to the poor women with whom they worked (God's Geese - Sisters of Charity). In Our day **Mother Theresa** of Calcutta did the same. This development was a tremendous step forward toward greater freedom, respect, and treating women as the Image of God. Women today, have free access to social work, hospital care, teaching, and even the field of law, theology, engineering, administration etc. because of the radical character of women's religious orders. They have pressed their case for the beauty of the feminine. It might well be today that the religious orders of women are waiting for another Louise de Marillac to bring about a revolution for women religious.

Cokie Roberts[47] in her delightful little book, points out the radical changes concerning women that came about in society as a result of World I and World II. It is said *"necessity is the mother of invention"*, it was a necessity that we have the WACs, the WAVEs, and ROSIE the Riveter. My sister, **Catherine,** was one of the first women meteorologist. During her training the government kept asking her for her high school diploma. She said it was in the mail. Finally her marks were such that they forgot about the diploma. She had only one year of high school.

---

[47] Cokie Roberts, "We are Our Mothers' Daughters", (William Morrow & Co. N.Y.) 1998. p.61-75. Roberts expresses very well what has happened, for good, to women during the period of her life. You might disagree with some of her insights, but I don't think you will find her disagreeable.

William L. Forst

What has emerged from all of this is quite astounding. Women performed very well, all were amazed at their abilities, that they could replace men in most occupations of life. The women were educated with the best of men. This has had great reverberation within the Church. We have women who are able to express their thoughts developed from their free conscience. We have **women theologians, philosophers and canonists**, all of whom are expressing delightfully different insights about the Church. These are exciting and exacting times. The first time this has ever happened within the Roman Catholic Church. However, so far, the official church institution has yet to announce the aesthetics of the feminine, even though the majority of theological students today are women.

With Vatican II great insights and changes occurred regarding women and married people. The marriage act is not seen as sinful but as a beautiful gift of God. An act where by husband and wife experiences the power of God's Spirit. It certainly fulfills the requirements for a sacrament. The purpose of marriage is a relationship of love and support of one another. With these changes the women's place is moving toward a greater equality with her male partner. Today the present problem that faces the Church, which may be the 2nd greatest problem the Church has ever faced - ***"What are we going to do with the women?"*** I think the greatest problem the church dealt with was, ***"What are we going to do with the Gentiles?"*** (Acts 15:19-30). The problem with women is so difficult and complex for there are many issues that spin around women. For instance, the matter of power: how will it be shared, what form will it take, will the leaders be called upon to be servants and possess compassion, and in what manner will power be structured? Also the other matter of sexual ethics will have to be dealt with. The Church's overly strict understanding of sexual morality will be challenged. To say nothing of the whole idea of ordination of women to the priesthood.

It appears that God values an institution and organization according to the respect that is given to women. If there is respect given to women the institution supports aesthetics and will find a place for beauty. If the institution does not respect women there will be no place for aesthetics. We saw the Taliban government of Afghanistan that looks upon women with great disrespect. Because of this it can harbor cutthroats and terrorists, and even approves and supports their activity. There is no place for aesthetics in the government. This, of course, is an extreme. Jesus clearly stated the principal here, *"One can not love two masters"* - one who loves God and a master that rejects the beauty of God's creation. Women are, after all, one half the population of the human race. We believe as Christians she is (as Adam is) God's image and equal to man.

From Augustine to Teilhard de Chardin represents more than 1800 years of progress regarding women:

> *"Man does many things with the fire that burns in his heart. He gathers power, pursues glory, creates beauty, devotes himself to science. And often he does not realize that, under so many different forms, it is always the same*

passion that inspires him - purified, transformed, but alive - the attraction of the Feminine"[48]

Beauty and aesthetics of the women is displayed as a special gift she has in being a co-creator with God of human life. Her dignity comes from being God's Image, and she, with the Mother of Jesus, is deserving of the priesthood. The Church will be far superior as it honors and respects her in word as well as in deed.

Aesthetics as Diversity, Diversity as Beauty

"Only by venturing into the unknown do we enable new ideas to take shape, and those shapes are different for each voyager." Margaret J. Wheatley

What God has wrought in the 1st chapter of the Hebrew Bible (Genesis) is diversity. All of creation is diverse, and God said, **'all that I created is good'.** There is diversity in the human, animal and the inanimate world in which we live. The Greeks and the world of Aristotle thought of the entire cosmos as a vast living organism. Today we call it a holistic vision. About a hundred years ago Rene Descartes, Isaac Newton, and others expressed their vision of a machinelike world, governed entirely by universal mathematical laws, which left very little room for spontaneity or freedom. They eliminated, or did not recognize, a great deal of the original diversity,

---

[48] Ursula King, "Spirit of Fire", Orbis Books, NY. 1998, p.75

but saw the world as static. The Industrial Revolution grew up with this view; the human worker becomes a machine. The Popes of the 20th century have tried to change this.

Modern Quantum science is agreeing with the mystics of old that **all of creation is related**, and all of creation is good. This diversity within creation enhances the fantastic beauty. This beauty that God has wrought needs to be protected by the churches of the world. Many theologians have written about this matter and it's importance. I mention only a few: Hans Kung, Teilhard de Charden, and Denis Edwards.[49] Dominican Richard Woods[50] says about all this:

> *"The undeniable fact that Earth is being systematically rendered unfit to sustain life today is a blasphemous affront to the Creator of life and thus constitutes a profound challenge to both Christian theology and spirituality. In the coming decades, any spirituality that does not address itself actively to the healing of the earth on both the individual and corporate level, to the alleviation of the suffering of the wretched of the earth by works of social justice, and to the unification of the human family and the world of nature in love and compassion, will to that extend become irrelevant."*

---

[49] Hans Kung, "A Global Ethic for Global Politics and Economics", Oxford University Press, NY 1998: Teihard de Chardin - by Ursula King, "Spirit of Fire", Orbis Books, NY 1996: Denis Edwards, "Jesus the Wisdom of God", Orbis Books, NY

[50] Richard Woods, "The Seven Bowls of Wrath: An Ecological Parable," Ecotheology 7 (1999): 8-21

William L. Forst

A Servant leader will certainly pay great attention to the vast diversity that exists in all of creation. This diversity exists in the various religions, cultures, and traditions of the world. We then can see that all of creation is the beauty of God.

Pneuma Artist Bill Forst

Chapter # 3

Moral is attracted to Goodness – p. 73
Goodness as Ethics – p. 74
Prophecy the Core of the Moral – p. 77
Moral Act Requires Freedom – p. 83
Moral Recognizes Human Dignity – p. 90
The Morality and Goodness of a Franchise Parish – p. 91
Moral as Related to Law – p. 97

Moral is attracted to Goodness

We all need 'moral goodness' in our lives as well as truth, beauty, and unity. There are secure connections between these transcendentals. There is no doubt that the transcendentals- truth - beauty - goodness - unity interacts and relate mutually with one another. I am sure that if I discard truth, I am also saying farewell to goodness and beauty. All are very important for us **"to love the neighbor as oneself"**. Without tending to these transcendentals, ones spirituality will be of little worth. Truth, Beauty and Goodness are absolutely necessary if we are to have healthy relations with others, and if we are to live in a life-giving community, if we are to have unity. To live with the transcendentals is to live as a human being as well as we are capable of living. The Catholic Church must make it a point to articulate these transcendentals with the People of God.

William L. Forst

Goodness as Ethics

"Obscene is not the picture of a woman who exposes her pubic hair, but that of a fully clad general who exposes his medals rewarded in a war of aggression; obscene is not the ritual of the hippies but the declaration of a high dignitary of the church that war is necessary for peace." Herbert Marcuse

Aristotle developed ethics, as a branch of philosophy. Ethics is called a science, because it is concerned with human conduct, as distinguished from the formal sciences, such as mathematics and logic, and the empirical sciences, such as chemistry and physics. Ethics has a close relationship to psychology and the social sciences. **So the concern of Ethics is the attainment of social harmony.** A harmony in human relationships so that each person can attain the development of her/his highest gifts, each being productive in such a manner that these gifts are shared with the community. The big question is how do we balance the needs of the individual with the needs of the community. I'm sure this is the kind of ethics that Jesus produced when he said, *"You are to love your neighbor as yourself"*. Vatican Council II (Modern World 17) says it so concisely and clearly, *"Only in freedom can a person direct themselves toward goodness."*

The ethics of Confucius is described as a *yen*. *Yen* is translated as "**love**" or *"goodness," "humanity,"* or even *"human-heartiness"*. *Yen* is a virtue representing human qualities at their best. In human relations, construed as those between one person and another, *yen* is manifested in *chung*, or faithfulness to oneself and others, and *shu*, or altruism, best expressed in the Confucian golden rule, **"Do not do to others what you do not want done to yourself."** One sees the close resemblance of Confucius to Aristotle, and later to Jesus. I suspect that Jesus was aware of these two philosophers.

Presently large companies around the world are hiring Ethics Officers. An Ethics Officers Association was formed in 1992 with 12 members, now the association has 507 members. An Ethic code for a company is not a rulebook, but *'it's what is and what isn't the spirit of the company'*. Texas Instruments, Levi Strauss & Co., Bell South Corp., Hewlett Packard, United Technologies, and many more are finding out that ethics is cost effective. These companies have adopted ethics codes, ethics officers, and ethics training.[51] The ethics officers take care of the following: conflict of interest situations in the company, when a company moves out of a town and accepts responsibility for the people of the town, the presence of bribing in a company, when a manager 'chews out an employee' in an abusive manner, and many more situations. Companies are finding out that integrity, trust, truth, and compassion are very important, and certainly a part of the companies business.

"We have created a culture in which there's no distinction between what is illegal and what is unethical."
Zbigniew Brezezinski

---

[51] The Christian Science Monitor, August 10, 1998, B1

However not all companies are cleaning up their act. A recent article in the St. Louis Post Dispatch[52] tells of shady practices of four large companies: **Solutia's** pollution problems, Tyson's immigration problems with six of it's managers, Enron's accounting problems and then bankruptcy, and Ford's safety problems. Also troubling in business unethical activities are cases where executives learned of problems and either failed to move on them, or tried to cover up the difficulty. The cover up in our Church scandal activities. In these situations (especially church) good ethics can save a great deal of money.

In all of this, it might be well to come up with a short attractive statement that might serve as a bumper sticker. It could be a catchy little statement that would immediately capture a person's imagination. The Buddhist put it in these words, *"Seek for others the happiness you desire for yourself"*, today's teens say, *"WWJD"* or *"What would Jesus Do?"* I like these statements because they say it all. Ethics is being affected by every person in the world. Treating persons with compassion. When we do this it shapes up our own life as well. For we learn to love ourselves as we love one another. We can not do any of this unless we bring about ethical actions in our own life. No easy task. This is ethics.

---

[52] Carey, Christopher, St. Louis Post Dispatch, "Business Ethics", January 6, 2002, B1

Prophecy the Core of the Moral

"I have a dream that my four little children will one day live in a nation where they will not be judged by the color of their skin but by the content of their character. I have a dream today." Martin Luther King Jr.

Prophecy is absolutely essential to moral activity that leads to goodness. Socrates is a prophet even though he did not consider himself one. He received the treatment that many prophets receive. He was abused and misunderstood by the power people of his time, and went to his death on the false charge of 'corrupting the youth'. Jesus, the prophet, was also given capitol punishment, of the cross, for asking his church and government to be more truthful and compassionate. Many of the present churches in the western world are so blotched by consumerism and materialism that the prophetic voice is all but squelched.

There are many texts in the scriptures, both the Hebrew and Christian scriptures that show the vital importance of the prophetic message. The Hebrew Scriptures (Old Testament) spins around the prophets. As today, they had good and bad prophets. Let us speak only of one Micah who made the famous prophecy. A sculpture of this prophecy sits in front of the United Nations, and was created and donated by Russia. The Sculpture portrays the words of Micah 4:1-4,

"He will rule over the nations and settle disputes for many peoples. They will beat their swords into plowshares and their spears into pruning hooks. Nation will not raise

> *sword against nation: neither will they train for war any more. But each one will sit in peace and freedom under a fig tree or a vine of his own, for the mouth of Yahweh of hosts has spoken."*

At the United Nations Pope Paul VI said **"No More War"**. An intense prophesy, but who pays attention - even among the churches? Many wars today are religious wars: Northern Ireland - Protestant Vs Catholic; Bosnia - Orthodox, Vs Christian, Vs Muslin; Near East, Jew, Vs Muslin, Vs Christian, Vs Orthodox, now in Afghanistan, and in Iraq. If religions preached and lived *'love one another'*, the wars would stop. It was Albert Einstein, the great scientist, who said you couldn't simultaneously prevent and prepare for war. On one hand the USA spends billions of dollars preparing for war, selling weapons of destruction to many other nations, also enslaving our own people in prisons, and fostering the legal killing machine of death penalty and abortion. Presently our country is carrying on a war against terrorist. This is an oxymoron, for all wars are terrorism.

On the other hand USA speaks quite openly that we are a Christian and peace loving country. We even have a President who uses the word **'compassion'** regarding his politics. Where are the religions in bringing real peace among nations? They are sitting on the sidelines building multimillion-dollar ministry plants with some of the money coming from the war effort.

According to Megan McKenna[53] Micah (the prophet) gives us the moral and ethical code for Israel: *"You have been told, O man, what is good and what Yahweh requires of you: to do justice, to love mercy, and to walk humbly with God (Mic 6-8)."* This is the bottom line of a prophet. *'Do justice'*, is not just an act of justice but also a whole life style of living and breathing justice? *'To Love mercy'*, is compassion and tenderness to the poor, aliens, and the outcasts of the world. The impartial and unconditional love God has for his people must be lived. *'Walk humbly with your God'*, we are to stand in awe to God's power, God's goodness, this is present in everything that we do. The prophetic message today is very much needed in the churches of the west.

The time after Jesus lived, prophets were considered on the same level as apostles (Eph 4:11). Today prophets should be considered on the same level as bishops and the pope. Many people considered Jesus a prophet. However this was difficult for Jesus to accept since prophets were considered at a flunky level by the church leaders of his time (Mt. 13:57, Acts 13:26-27). The leaders even indicated that Galilee was not the place of prophets (Jn. 7,52). Jesus indicated that he did not come to abolish the prophetic message but to fulfill it (Mt. 5:17). The making of the gospel cannot be done without the prophetic message. This is true for the church of all time. However, today, it is common for the Church to reject the prophets, to insult them, to move them away from the accepting people.

---

[53] Megan McKenna, "The Prophet", Orbis Books, NY, 2001 p. 128-132

William L. Forst

Rabbi Abraham Joshua Heschel[54] says,

> prophets ***"are some of the most disturbing people who have ever lived: the men whose inspiration brought the Bible into being - the men whose image is our refuge in distress, and whose voice and vision sustain our faith."***

A prophet speaks the word of the lord. Many prophetic messages in the Hebrew Scriptures were introduced by ***"Thus says the Lord"***. Megan McKenna[55] says ***"The prophet is a truth-teller, using the power of God to shatter the silence that surrounds injustice."*** I like this because, today, telling the truth is such a difficult gesture to make for large, bureaucratic, international institutions and for the people who work in these institutions. Here I include the Roman Catholic Church, for the church bureaucracy in its present drive for power and control, attempts to control prophecy as well.

The church has a difficult time recognizing prophets because prophets are usually mysteries. They have intensity and a drive to speak God's word. They generally do not fulfill the various protocol that modern institutions demand. They don't operate within canon law. They are not an inner part of the institution. They are modern day '**whistle-blowers**' and, as in Jesus time, no one approves of whistle blowers or prophets, especially the institutions which whistle is being blown.

---

[54] Abraham Heschel, 'The Prophets: an Introduction", Harper and Row, NY, 1962 ix
[55] Ibid. Megan McKenna, p. 19

A great prophet for our time is Bishop Samuel Ruiz of San Cristobal de Las Casas, Chiapas, Mexico. Presently he, like many of us, is retired, but his 'word' lives on. As a young priest he was appointed Bishop of San Christobal in 1960. At first, he says, I did not notice how these people were oppressed by the government and by the church. Gradually Dom Samuel (as they called him) began to assert himself into the Mayan culture, and gradually inculturated the western Roman church into the Church of the Mayan people. For hundreds of years the missionaries have been (still are) inculterating the Mayan people into the western church. It has taken us 100s of years to realize that this is not evangelization. This is not respecting the freedom of one's conscience. Dom Samuel spoke of what happen:

> *"What all world cultures have is a revealing presence of God, what the Greek and Latin Fathers called the seeds of the word -* **semina verbi** *- hidden in cultures. In consequence, evangelization (and inculturation) is not - forgive the expression- an attempt to determine how many goals from your culture (western - Roman) you can score in the indigenous culture. The object is rather to recognize the presence of a salvific process..."*[56]

Dom Samuel continued to recognize the beautiful traditions and liturgies these people had developed over 100s of years in their clan and tribe structure (true of African peoples today). These people are not pagan, but have dynamic belief in God, and powerful liturgies

---

[56] Gary MacEoin, "Seeds of the Word", National Catholic Reporter, Feb. 8, 2000 p.10

to express that belief. The Mayan culture must be inculterated into the Western Roman Church.

As I write this, I often wonder just how long it will take the USA Bishops to recognize this very thing among the people of the USA? We have our own prophets, our own culture and traditions, which are very different from the Roman Culture. When will our **Bishops be prophets** (as Bishop Ruiz) and reject the Vatican's attempts to control: how we run our great catholic university system, how we use the English language in our liturgy, how we come to a solution of the priest problem, how we fix the woman problem, what are we going to do about celibacy, even how we elect our own bishops, etc. The Bishops and the People of God are open to the Spirit of God. Cannot the Vatican trust the People of God in the USA? All of the concerns, I mentioned, could be and should be settled by the church of the USA. What we need are servant leaders willing to be prophetic. We need servant leaders (per Dom Samuel) not concerned about their power or position, not concerned about money or buildings, but only concerned about releasing the salvific power of Jesus to the people. Great things happen in the Church when we listen to prophets and the People of God.

Moral Act Requires Freedom

"Fear makes us ultimately vulnerable to domination while interior freedom makes us strong enough to face whatever needs to be faced without either temerity or cowardice." Sr. Sandra M. Schneiders

In the fall of 1997 I was watching an awards TV presentation for the best "Shows" of the past year. One award went to a director (who's name I did not catch). Later a TV interviewer asked this director a question. *"How do you excite an actor's creativity?"* And the director immediately said, *"I give them full freedom"*. The God given creativeness of any person, in any form can only be touched in a frame work of freedom. I thought to myself, which has to be a very Christian answer. It appears to me that the Holy Spirit cannot have her results except when the individual is functioning in freedom.

In our lives as Christian people we are forever being called upon to freely respond to the Spirit of God. Scripture says, time and again, our response cannot be forced or compelled; it will be true only in freedom. Paul says, 2 Cor 3:17

> *"Now the Lord is the Spirit, and where the Spirit of the Lord is, there is freedom." Gal 5:13 Paul utters, "For you were called to freedom, brethren; only do not use your freedom as an opportunity for the flesh, but through love be servants of one another."*

Paul was a man pushed by a demon to bring down the followers of Jesus. He approved of St. Steven's death by stoning. Paul, later in a framework of freedom, agreed to become the Apostle to the Gentiles (Acts 9:15), and this task proved to be very prophetic. Even though Paul was responding to the Spirit, his actions brought great change in the early church, as well as much torment and even violence to him. Paul's creativity would never have been touched if he did not respond to the Spirit of God in freedom. The early church gave Paul this freedom.

The same might be said of every Christian person. With Baptism we are given the freedom and responsibility to answer the Spirit of God in our life. The Spirit will guide us, but only in freedom. It is in this freedom that the beauty of our creativity will be stirred. Paul indicates that we all form one body, but the individual members perform their various tasks, and are always to freely use their *"gifts"* for the good of all. It is in this freedom that our creativity shows its beauty.

During the 300s, and when **'Caesaro-Papism'** (Caesar is Pope) began to show it's ugly face, the church began to be wrapped in the power of politics. It now was interested in making a place for it's self in the secular world. This proved to be a terrible temptation for the Church. There was great distress regarding the freedom to choose. The church now had political power to coerce and sometimes to force faith upon people. The Emperor wanted 'peace' in his kingdom. This rejection of freedom would grow, over hundreds of years, into the Crusades and the Inquisition. This was a time when

If Aristotle Ran the Catholic Church

the Church would deny freedom of religion and freedom of conscience. Vatican II, 1962 - 1965, has renewed freedom to the People of God.

> "You can't separate peace from freedom
> because no one can be at peace
> unless he has his freedom" Malcolm X

The document 'Religious Freedom' of Vatican II Council for the first time, in more than a thousand years, boldly declares the importance of freedom of conscience in matters of religion.

> *"All are bound to follow their conscience faithfully in every sphere of activity so that they may come to God, who is their last end. Therefore, the individual must not be forced to act against conscience nor be prevented from acting according to conscience, especially in religious matters. The reason is because the practice of religion of its very nature consists primarily of those voluntary and free internal acts by which human being direct themselves to God. (11)This truth appears at its height in Christ Jesus, in whom God manifests Himself, (Rm 14:12; cf. Rm 14:1-23; 1 Cor 8:9-13; 10:23-33) and for that reason is bound to obey his conscience(3)."*

The following is another text that supports the dignity of the human conscience wherein lies the beauty of human creativity, all within the setting of freedom. This text is taken from Church in the Modern World, section No. 16.

> *"Deep within their consciences men and women discover a law which they have not laid upon themselves and which they must obey. Its voice, ever calling them to love and to do what is good and to avoid evil, tells them inwardly at the right moment: do this, shun this. For they have in their hearts a law inscribed by God. Their dignity rests in observing this law, and by it they will be judged (Rom. 2:14-16). Their conscience is people's most secret core, and their sanctuary. There they are alone with God whose voice echoes in their depths".*[57]

This says a great deal about the dignity of the human being, no matter what religion, or color, or race, or what sex, or where that person may live in the world. It is based upon the conscience that we all possess, and that conscience runs at the very center of our life. Conscience is the secret place in which we meet our God. Our conscience can only be exercised in **freedom**.

It is interesting to know that the council has a real difficult time getting the Decree on Religious Freedom accepted. This went on for two or three years during the council. I quote from my brother, **Marion,** as he speaks about it in his Journal:[58]

> *"We adjourned in time to have a drink and dinner about 7:30pm. As we sat at the table, Bishop John Wright and Bishop James Griffith circulated to say that in a meeting of the Theological Commission that they had just attended, by a vote of 18 to 5, authorization was provided for the*

---

[57] See Pius XII, radio message on rightly forming the Christian conscience in youth, 23 March 1952:AAS 44(1952), p.271
[58] Marion M. Forst, "Daily Journal of Vatican II", Forest of Peace Pub. Kansas City, KS, 2000, p. 72

admission of the chapter on Religious Freedom into the schema De Ecumenismis.

This was one of the great breakthroughs of the Council. Because the Commission was dominated by Curia traditionalists like Ottaviani and Browne, it meant a defeat of the Curia as well as their thinking. Fr. John Courtney Murray, S.J., suppressed by the Holy Office for his views on religious liberty, apparently gave a talk as a peritus on the subject, and, perhaps, helped bring the favorable vote."

Our country was founded upon the fact that people work best within a framework of freedom. Even though women and slaves were not considered free, this was a great advancement from what had gone before. The wonderful thing about the US Constitution is that it is not absolute or infallible, and because of that it is alive and can grow. It has been growing to the present time. Through war and political battles both Blacks and Women have made great progress in obtaining their freedom. The difficulty has always been in the sharing of power. The Constitution of Athens, in Aristotle's time, had the same problem - where does the power reside. Aristotle said the power and the vote resided with those who are rational and logical. Accordingly Aristotle excluded women and slaves.

'FREE AT LAST, FREE AT LAST. THANK GOD ALMIGHTY, WE ARE FREE AT LAST'
Martin Luther King Jr.

The Catholic Church down through the centuries has provided great inspiration for democracy, freedom, and respect for the dignity of the human being. The church has not always lived what it preached. In our country today, we live in a liberal democracy and many people are calling into question this matter of *'freedom'*. Stephen L. Carter takes great issue with what is happening to freedom in the USA. He recalls that the freedom to marry, is also a freedom to make a life commitment, to accept responsibility in good times and in bad, and a freedom to help our neighbors. But what seems to be happening is that people are accepting freedom as freedom from a commitment, from responsibility, from sacrifice, and a freedom from helping the neighbor.[59] I just received Issue 90 from the Southern Poverty Law Center that claims there are 523 *'Freedom'* patriot groups in our county, and 12 in Missouri alone. These groups generally view themselves as free to be racists and white supremacists. Is this really what freedom entails in our constitution?

Dr. Diana Hayes[60], an African American, says regarding freedom as it is desired by minority people in USA:

> *"I believe that my rights as an African American woman are guaranteed only when the rights of all are guaranteed; that my liberty is restricted when that of another is restricted; that my human dignity is denied when that of others is trampled into the dirt. I believe that no one can be free until all are free."*

---

[59] Carter, Stephen L. (Basic Books; 10 E. 53rd St. N.Y. 1998) p.71-84
[60] Elizabeth A. Johnson editor, Diana Hayes, "The Church Women Want", Crossroads Pub Co. NY.2002, p.91

The church and country has come a long way in the past 100 years, but both have a long way to go before we ever arrive at the freedom for which Jesus died.

The Church is forever fighting this battle for all people to be free. Vatican II document - Modern World, No.17 expresses in beautiful and powerful words:

> *"Genuine freedom is an exceptional sign of the image of God in humanity. For God willed that men and women should "be left free to make their own decisions" (Eccl 17: 7-8) ......Since human freedom has been weakened by sin it is only by the help of God's grace that people can properly orientate their actions towards God".*

We have seen that the church has upheld the need of 'freedom' in society, but down through the centuries it has had difficulty permitting freedom of expression to its theologians. We are aware that Church did not permit theological vision to Martin Luther, Savanarola, John Hus, **Galileo**, and many more. But can't the Church learn from past faults? Today we have a whole litany of the Church denying creativity and freedom to: Hans Kung, Charles Curran, Tissa Balasuriya, Taihard de Charden, John Courtney Murray, Bernard Haring, etc. I do believe the time is coming soon when the Church will permit freedom and creativity to its great theologians and scientists so that the work of Jesus can continue. Sr. Sandra M. Schneiders states:

> *"Fear makes us ultimately vulnerable to domination while interior freedom makes us strong enough to face*

whatever needs to be faced without either temerity or cowardice."[61]

Moral Recognizes Human Dignity

Human Beings are all created to God's Image Gen 1:27

Margaret Wheatley has written a classic book, "Leadership and the New Science".[62] She talks about systems that work well in physical science. All creation is in relationship. In the subatomic world (and in the real world) particles and people have the ability to 'self-reference' and 'self-organize'. These particles *'self-reference'* when there is change, they then can refer themselves to the right path for which they were designed. They do this in order to preserve themselves. These particles are able to *'self-organize'* themselves. Again there is change, fluctuation in the system and they have the ability to organize themselves, to bring order out of chaos. Both the 'self-referencing' and the self-organizing' ability is supported by a clear identity (they know themselves) and freedom.

Mr. Jantsch, a scientist, expresses this profound teaching in the human world in which we live today:

---

[61] Sandra M. Schneiders, "Finding the Treasure", Paulist Press, NY p.264
[62] Margaret Wheatley, "Leadership and the New Science", Berrett-Koehler Pub. San Francisco, 2nd Ed. 1999. This has to be a 'must' for leadership people.

> *"The natural dynamics of simple dissipative structures teach the optimistic principle of which we tend to despair in the human world: 'the more freedom, self-organization, the more order".*

This hits directly at the amazing dignity of the human being - we are the Image of God. When freedom is given us we can 'self-reference' ourselves, and we can very well 'self-organize' ourselves even within the Church. How long will it be before the Church realizes that the People of God have this amazing dignity and responsibility? When will the People of God demand this respect from the Church institution?

The Morality and Goodness of a Franchise Parish

> *"We Need Leaders to understand that we are best controlled by concepts that Invite Participation."*
> Margaret Wheatley

Webster's dictionary has several **definitions of franchise**. **#1** Freedom or immunity from some burden or restriction vested in a person or group. **#2** A special privilege granted to an individual or group. **#3** the right to exercise the powers of a corporation. The first can be looked upon as moral and good. The other definitions are very questionable from the moral point of view.

Concerning each definition of a franchise; **#1 Franchise** - a person, or organization that finds it bound up with the heavy restrictions, excommunication, suspensions, or punishment—these burdens must be removed by forgiveness. The franchise of forgiveness must be offered to anyone or any organization that has made a 'sinful' mistake. This is what happened to Peter and the 11 apostles who made the sinful act of rejecting Jesus. Peter, especially, because he was forewarned, freely accepted the responsibility, and then he buckled terribly and sinfully in denying Jesus. Jesus gave Peter a non-restricted franchise of forgiveness. It was this franchise that was so beautifully moral and good. It was this franchise that made Peter change and become the beautiful leader he was for the early Church - willing to grant the franchise of forgiveness to the gentiles, women, and slaves.

#2 Franchise - may be a privilege granted to a person or group. Granting privileges to one person over another can be very divisive. For one who believes that all human beings are the image of God, granting privileges to one and not to others is a violation of our equality. Or it is a violation of what Peter learned from Cornelius that **"God shows no partiality"** (Acts 10:34; Rm 2:11). To give the privilege, the franchise, of ordination to a male and not to a female is a dishonest policy. We learn in the first book of the Bible that male and female are equal before God.

#3 Franchise is the right to exercise the powers of a corporation. Take a look at the franchise method that has been used by the McDonald Food Corporation[63]. The first franchised corporations were Dunkin' Donuts and Kentucky Fried Chicken, but,

---

[63] Eric Schlosser, "Fast Food Nation", Houghton Mifflin, NY, 2001 P. 91-107

later, McDonald perfected the franchising technique. A franchise from a not too well known corporation, Grimby Pizza, may cost as little as $15,000. A Burger King franchise today runs about $1.5 million. However McDonald franchise costs about $500,000 but, unlike other franchises, the **McDonald Company** owns the property upon which the restaurant is built, giving them much greater control. The franchiser controls the size, shape, and looks of the building. There is a booklet of about 100 pages that regulates every aspect of running the franchise. There is no room for creativity, imagination for the franchisee. Even Federal law demands full disclosure prior to a sale, but does not regulate how franchises are run thereafter. Federal laws do not cover employees of the franchiser, and franchisees are not covered by laws that protect independent business persons. The fast food industries have lobbied hard and long with millions of dollars so that the federal government does not get involved. I ask you is this what Jesus would describe as justice? Is this a 'compassionate' manner of running a business? It may be legal, but is it moral and good?

The **modern Parish**, in USA, is run pretty much as a business franchise. The one big difference is the franchisee -Pastor - pays no money for the franchise. The people of the parish are those responsible for payment, or investment, to the franchiser - the bishop. The people have financial responsibilities but they receive few benefits. The people are not able to chose who will be their pastor (manager), they are not able to determine how long the pastor stays, and even the duties or obligations of the pastor. So even though the

People of God must pay for the franchise they have no say in the operation. The people must pay the pastor, but the pastor has a certain power over the people. The pastor and not the people are held responsible by the franchiser- the bishop. The parish is run by an elaborate set of guidelines - Canon Law (1700 canons) and diocesan laws. As with McDonalds, the land upon which the parish buildings are built is owned and controlled by the franchiser - the bishop. The parish franchise seems worse, than McDonalds, in that the pastor and the people of God have little or no ability to use their god given gifts of creativity and imagination. Also the manner in which the pastor and people of God contact the Spirit of God is controlled by the man made laws (Canon Law). An article recently in the Monitor[64] reporting on the general finances of the American Catholic Church says it will not go bankrupt, says Anson Shupe, sociologist, **"It's like McDonald's there is no one Catholic church in the United States, They are all separate corporate entities - a bunch of franchises."**

I am well aware that under the present circumstances many priests, pastors, and people of God simply do not abide by the directives of the franchiser. But the point - is the present large suburban parish moral? Does this large parish encourage Servant Leadership? Is this type of parish capable of building community? Has the franchise parish been wrapped in the trappings of a consumerist, fast-paced, individualistic culture? Are the People and

---

[64] Christian Science Monitor, "Scandals will dent, not bankrupt, dioceses," By Mark Clayton, March 28, 2002, P. 3

Pastor free to respond to the Spirit of God in running their parish? Is the Pastor of this large parish a CEO?

The pastor is obligated to get the money to run these businesses (Disney theme park) with beautiful schools, modern sports facilities, wedding chapels, offices for the bureaucratic theme organizers. A parish is measured by its profit. An article by Robert Kress,[65] says a serious consequence for priest-pastors is a sort of schizophrenia. Kress mentions two pastor friends of his one says, **"I hate all this administration"**, and the other states **"They didn't tell us about this in the seminary."** This must be one reason why so many priests are refusing to be pastors. One of our pastors having spent many years in Peru, and now back involved with an American parish says, **"I am not a fund raiser"**. One great accolade given to Archbishop Rigali, now moved to Philadelphia, is **"He is a great fund raiser"**. He now is at the height of the competition.

In the September issue of **'New Oxford Review'**[66] a conservative magazine, titles an article "The Second Greatest Scandal in the Church.' The author is a retired (many great reports come from the retired) federal law enforcement official. He devised a procedure that can monitor the weekend collections of parish churches. Website www.ChurchSecurity.info He cites the millions of dollars that are being stolen from the Sunday collections. The article reveals,

---

[65] Robert Kress, America, "The Priest-Pastor As C.E.O.", March 11, 2002 p. 8
[66] Michael W. Ryan, "New Oxford Review" September 2003 p. 23

> *'a surprisingly clear and shocking connection between the hierarchy's laissez-faire attitude toward revenue protection and the ability of preditor-preists to fund their deviant activities.'*

Secrecy that was used with the sex scandal is also being exploited to cover up this financial scandal. Our leaders are saying 'forget about it' it could not happen within the Catholic Church. These franchise parishes are acting like any other franchise.

There doesn't seem to be any effective manner of measuring the depth of faith in a parish. The Sunday envelope is the bottom line measurement. The profit producing parishes must build and maintain large business complexes. Dr. Dean Hoge[67] of Catholic University Washington DC says, **"The concept of bankruptcy does not apply here."** An estimate by Joseph C. Harris[68] puts revenue for 19,000 catholic parishes and 8,300 schools nationwide at $13.2 billion.

To pay the diocesan bureaucrats (different from parish bureaucrats) there is the **Cathadraticum,** which is a tax the diocese assesses on the people of the parishes to pay the operation of the chancery. In the last 40 years this tax has gone through the roof. Each diocese has its system. Generally this tax is skewed to benefit the larger (rich) parishes. A Parish with a debt and a school will get a tax relief for the debt and school. Small parishes, with a debt, will get the debt relief, but the larger parishes will have a larger debt and school for a greater piece of tax relief. The parish without a school

---

[67] Ibid
[68] Ibid

(smaller or poor parish) must pay a tax penalty. This amounts to the poor parishes supporting the richer parishes. This diocesan dynamic is the same that is happening in our economic community- the rich are getting richer and the poor are getting poorer. Like business, if there is no profit the poor parish will be closed (many have been closed in the inner city and rural). Jesus' ministry was to the outcasts of the society, the poor, the imprisoned, and the lepers. But it seems we have developed a parish system where the outcasts are the last to be served. So it appears that the Parish as a franchise and a business needs a great deal of healing attention.

Moral as Related to Law

"If you are led by the Spirit you are not under the law."
Gal 5:18
"Extreme Law is often extreme injustice" Terence 163 BC

Philosophers have grappled down through the centuries as to the place of law in the work of morality. In my place of residence (a HUD subsidized housing, well run by the Archdiocese of St. Louis) I have gone down to the front desk and sometimes find a person obediently tending the door and phone, many times passing time by playing solitary. I have asked, *'Are you winning?'* and frequently I get the answer with some humility, *'No, I never win'*, and I translate that into *'I am a loser'*. I usually say to the person *'you make the rules of the game, and therefore you should always win.'* At times I get the false humility when one says *'I never cheat'*. I am not asking them to cheat but to be in control of their life. I realize that if I play solitary on the computer, there is no chance for me 'to cheat' for the rules are embedded (as the journalists were embedded in the Iraq war) in the computer. I have no control over the rules, and so I will lose more times than I deem necessary.

I do resist when a human, fallible person programs a silly game in such a manner that this game says *'I am a loser'*. Even the liturgy of the Mass, which is described as a **'love feast'**, the bureaucrats are making rules as to when we are to bow, how to give the sign of peace, etc. Has it come to this; that we must follow rules in our love life? I think control over the slobs in being expressed. I understand in Christian life we must deal with the only law Jesus made for us is *'love the neighbor as self'*. We regard this law as absolute, since it was made by God. There are only winners with this law. With God there are no losers.

The present leadership of the church has to do with **making people losers**. The church has made a ton of laws, all of which are fallible. Many of these laws are not user-friendly, for the users have nothing to do with composing these laws. Besides the church makes laws behind a backdrop of infallibility, they also threaten punishment of hell if there is a violation. When Peter violated the infallible law of 'LOVE", Jesus asked Peter three times -*'Do you love me Peter?'* I do believe the whole system of law in the church needs drastic reform. To say the least it is not user-friendly.

How often we hear that morality cannot be legislated. It is helpful to look at what Jesus did regarding the law. Jesus knew that the making one law only demands the making two or three more. For Jesus gave one simple rule, and beyond that he put trust in the people. Jesus believed in the freedom of conscience, he did not believe in forcing rules upon his people. In Mark 12:28-34, a religious leader asked, **"Which is the First commandment of the all commandments"**? Jesus gives a very simply answer that we can make very complex. Jesus said:

> **"The first is, `Hear, O Israel: The Lord our God, the Lord is one; and you shall love the Lord your God with all your heart, and with all your soul, and with all your mind, and with all your strength.'** Then Jesus says the second is, `*You shall love your neighbor as yourself.' There is no other commandment greater than these.*"

Jesus says there is no other commandment that is more important than these. In fact all laws of church and state should in some way proceed from these two. It is interesting that Jesus never gave a set of laws for the operation of what we call today the institutional Church, or how the institutional church is to govern itself. The presumption is that it would govern itself by these two laws. He did in fact attempt to call his church to obedience of the two basic laws, and paid little or no attention to the 613 laws based on the Torah. Now the institutional Roman Catholic Church has made over 1700 laws (Canon Law), some even binding under pain of grave mortal (hell bent) punishment. And yet we still say morality cannot be legislated. I can only imagine what Jesus might do today if he returned to view the operation of many Churches that bear his name.

Somehow Paul also was trusting in the deep faith of the early Christians, he does not want them to get all involved figuring out the dos and don'ts of laws. If they keep the One Law, it would keep them. And I have come to this belief in my later life and wisdom that all human law must always be interpreted and understood with love, and then one must act accordingly.

When laws become complex and intricate they take away imagination and the responsibility of our conscience. God holds each of us responsible for our salvation not the law. Paul says laws take away the Spirit of God (Gal 5:18). Paul in Gal 5: 13-14 says very beautifully that we are all called to freedom, but freedom with responsibility. Then he mentioned the responsibility that the whole law is fulfilled in one phrase, *"You shall love your neighbor as yourself."* In Romans 3:20-21 Paul makes it clear where he stands regarding the law, and I guess we can apply this to all human law. Paul says:

> *"For no human being will be justified in his sight by works of the law, since through the law comes knowledge of sin. But now the righteousness of God has been manifested apart from law, although the law and the prophets bear witness to it."*

We all need freedom to respond to the Spirit of God. If rules and laws become so pervasive and omnipresent - then the prophetic Spirit cannot speak to us. To lose the prophetic voice is to lose Hope within the Church. To lose hope is to lose Christian imagination, thus to lose progress.

In speaking of imagination Bishop Sims[69] uses the story of the development of the caterpillar. At the approach of 'turning point' from caterpillar to butterfly, cells develop in the caterpillar's body called 'imaginal cells'. These cells provide the 'New vision and new beginnings' for the new life of the butterfly. The old clumsy, slow, ugly animal develops cooperatively into the new beautiful, cheerful, master of flight. All this because of 'imaginal cells'. The imagination in the human being (as imaginal cells) is a beautiful gift of God. It must be encouraged in an atmosphere of freedom. The Spirit of God works in this imagination to deliver the new. This new is a resurrection from an old, ponderous, bound up in law institution, to a new fresh, delightful, flight of God's Spirit. Imagination is the bottom line of hope, and hope depends on love and faith.

In writing about morality as it relates to law it is very important to be able to answer some questions about law. **Who makes the laws?** For whom are the laws made? Under what circumstances are these laws made? Whom do the laws oblige, and who are not obliged? Are there any exceptions to the law? **Is change built into the law making process?** Additions and amendments can make a simple rule, *'love the neighbor as yourself'* very complex, and we then find ourselves asking ***"Who is our Neighbor?."*** Now we need some one to interpret the law. Who then has the power of

---

[69] Bennett J. Sims, "Servanthood", (Cowley Pub., Cambridge MA.1997) p. 125

interpretation? Now we must figure out the How, Who, When, Where of law, and bango we have another book of law interpretation. The more laws we make the less trust we put in the faith of people of God.

The early church pretty well got rid of the **Mosaic Law with all its strange interpretations**. The early church built up it own law, and when Constantine took over in the 300s, the church pretty well adopted Roman Law as it's own. This built into a great volume of law, until the first codification of this bulk of law in 1917. At that time a procedure was put in place for a continual updating of this 1917 code, that procedure was never used. In 1959 Pope John XXIII not only called a Council, but also announced the revision of the Code of Canon Law. This was finished and duly promulgated in 1983. The number of laws was considerably decreased to 1752 laws by number. And this brings us back to what Jesus and Paul did - boiled all laws down to one essential law -*"Love the Neighbor as you love yourself'*. Remembering what Terence **said, 'Extreme Law is often extreme injustice.'**

**The symbols of Royalty need to go
We are a Church of the Poor**

Chapter # 4

The Spiritual generates Unity – p. 103
Unity with Diversity – p. 107
Unity as uniqueness – p. 117
Spirituality as Listening Brings Unity – p. 123
Spirituality is Friendship – p. 126
Spirituality Makes the Servant Leader – p. 130
Servant Leader Evokes Community – p. 133
Spirituality is Our Work – p. 138

The Spiritual generates Unity

WHAT IS A FRIEND? A SINGLE SOUL DWELLING IN TWO BODIES. Aristotle

Spirituality and unity are both sides of a coin; you can't have one without the other. Loves makes these two possible. Where there is true spirituality there will be unity between people, families, enemies, and nations. On the other hand, where there is no unity there is no trust and spirituality is improbable. Scientifically, it is being proven that unity exists in matter and in the cosmos. This is a change from Newtonian science. Fr. Teihard de Chardin,[70] as a young priest and scientist, began to realize the amazing unity within the world of matter and spirit. During World War I in the midst of terrible destruction of life and matter, his vision became clarified. He saw how matter was charged with life and spirit. He was beginning to

---

[70] Ursula King, "Spirit of Fire", (Orbis Books, Maryknoll, N.Y. 1998) p.53-58

understand that all matter, organic, psychic, or mental was connected to the fibers of our being. He believed that all human beings were in a process of forming a higher unity, not merely of individuals but a ***"communion with God through earth"***. The irony of it all this was that the treachery World War I stirred in Teihard a great mystical vision so that he would write and think about the ***"God-of-evolution"*** and the ***"Cosmic Christ."*** All of this brings unity. The scientist Brian Swimme[71] says, ***"No two particles [in the universe] can be considered disconnected, ever"***. This is the unity that God gave to the world. We find our spirituality in this unity.

It is our task as rational and willful human beings to bring this unity about where we live; family, school, business, and even among the churches. The disunity among the churches is a contributing cause for the many wars today. This is a monstrous scandal of our time. Vatican II[72] says in clear terms, this ***"division openly contradicts the will of Christ, scandalizes the world, and damages the sacred cause of preaching the Gospel to every creature"***. The churches are the institutions that preach compassion, forgiveness and acceptance. There is a loud cry that these churches join in unity, especially the Christian Churches. It appears that the big obstacle is the disposition of power. In January 1964 Pope Paul VI and the Patriarch Athenagoras met for the first time since 1439 and canceled the excommunication, going back to **1054**, that each church had on

---

[71] Brian Swimme and Thomas Berry, "The universe Story", (San Francisco: HarperCollins, 1992), 78
[72] Document on Ecumenism no. 1

the other. This was a start. Since then we have had the splitting of theological hairs in dogma, and lot a window dressing, but no unity. The unity among Christians, and other religions, is a matter of spirituality and not religion. Religion is about dogma, moral, liturgy, power, and property. Spirituality is intuitive and relational and concerned with love, compassion and forgiveness. We will never have unity among religions until these religions acquire a deep spirituality.

There are many beautiful faith filled families and singles that are searching diligently and eagerly in their relationship with God and one another. This is their spirituality. They are pushing themselves spiritually, but for many of them their religion has become an obstacle, at least not a help. Some have all but rejected a particular religion as a way of spiritual development. What are being rejected in these religions are legalism, exclusiveness, dogmatism and clericalism. These all express a lack of trust for the People of God. Without trust there is no unity nor is there spirituality.

I recently read a meaningful story that explains my present (retired) situation. Rachel Remen M.D tells the story[73] who describes a relationship between father and son. The two climb mountains together, and come down the other side of the mountain apart. The father observed that he remembers many of these climbs, but has no memory of what my son said or what I said to my son. In child psychology this is called 'parallel play' they are in the same sand box

---

[73] Rachel Naomi Remen, M.D. "Kitchen Table Wisdom", Riverhead Books, NY, 1996 p.157

lost in play, but they do not relate to one another. This parallel play goes on in families - spouse with spouse and with children. They might even share the act of intercourse with one another, but it is only a physical act and they continue not to know one another.

Remen asked the question *"is it possible to be lonely in the midst of family?"* I ask is it possible to be lonely as a priest with two brothers who are priests? Is it possible to be lonely in a church one loves which is dedicated to the truth and love? Is it possible to be lonely in a parish rectory (priest home) where there are two or more priests living? The answer to these questions might give us a clue to the problem of sexual abuse among priests as was exposed (March 2002). Remen says too often even among physicians and patients, the focus is on the disease and not on the patient. In developing our spirituality we really need to learn **how to love**, even love the enemy. Loneliness exists when we cannot communicate with the people with whom we live. This also spells disunity within a family and a lack of spirituality.

The People of God today are searching fearlessly for a spirituality that expresses a commitment to Jesus, a spirituality that can pattern our life with the life of Jesus. A spirituality that will be inclusive *"loving the neighbor as we love ourselves."* A spirituality that brings unity among all religions. They desire a religion in which the People of God are able to share their love, receive strength and direction from the community of lovers, and finally bring peace and unity to their little world of every day life. Aristotle said, *"What is a friend? A single soul dwelling in two bodies."*

Unity within Diversity

"When a Butterfly Flutters its wings in Tokyo, it can eventually cause a Tornado in St. Louis"
'Butterfly effect' by Ed Lorenz -and Chaos Theory-all things are related

There is diversity in every aspect of life, spiritual, psychological, physical, and human. This diversity is not to be considered a duality of right and wrong, or good or bad. The diversity of homosexual and heterosexual needs to be considered as God created them - diverse, 'either-or' rather than 'good-evil'. The only manner in which this marvelous diversity (God's creation) can survive is within the spirituality of unity. Deepak Chopra[74] says, *"Good is the union of all opposites. Evil no longer exists".* This is pretty much the same that Jesus said, *"Love your enemies"*, or that *"God is love".* If we love the enemy, the enemy no longer exists. If we love, then evil no longer exists. Unity has no limitations for it comes from God. Paul says, [1 Cor 15:56] *"The sting of death is sin, and the power of sin is the law."* Paul also says the foundation of law is love, [Gal 5:14] *"For the whole law is fulfilled in one word, "You shall love your neighbor as yourself".* This sets up the case that the bottom line of spirituality is love, and love alone can bring unity. Law is not the same as love.

---

[74] Deepak Chopra, "How to know God", Three Rivers Press, NY, 2000, p.170

And yet in face of the diversity of God's creation - we continue to make false boundaries and limitations (laws) in order for us to play God and say A is right and B is wrong, or to say Communism is an evil empire and USA is Christian. Books are written to show that the **Lutherans** belief in 'consubstantiation' is harmful, against the Roman Catholics that say 'transubstantion' is correct. There are those who swear on a stack of bibles that there is no 'Trinity", while others will argue that the 'Trinity' exists. Some make great arguments that Muslim is the true religion, while Judaism is false religion. We all know of the amazing diversity there is in religions of the world. We must investigate and accept the good that exists in all religions? The amazing diversity of religions must bring unity. It will bring unity when we can accept 'either-or' rather than 'good-evil'.

The above shows how easy it is to create opposites, or how to invent enemies, or to construct laws that say A is wrong and B is right. It was because of this fact that Jesus said, ***"Love your enemy"***. It doesn't make a hill of beans whether one is Muslin or Christian. Keeping a duality good vs. evil only breeds war and hatred. Certainly good vs. evil is behind the September 11th bombing of the Trade Center in New York. Unity comes when we are able to eliminate opposites or when opposites unite. The only thing that matters is love. Love evaporates differences.

This past century is the first time the Roman Catholic Church has become a global church. The great problem for the church today is accepting it's global responsibility. It no long is the Church of

Rome. We are no longer Roman Catholics but Universal Christians. This is what Jesus dreamt of from the very first. Vatican II (1965) pushed the church to be inculturated globally, and indicating that this is a harsh problem for the Church's Servant Leaders today. Roger Haight[75] expresses this beautifully:

> ***"Jesus Christ must become African, Indian, Sri Lankan, Filipino, and Bolivian, in the same measure in which he (Jesus) became Greek and Latin, and profoundly was reinterpreted by successive waves of western culture."***

Servant Leaders will recognize this amazing diversity of countries, cultures and religions and be skillful and clever enough to bring these people together in peace and love. But one's religion must not be an obstacle. God is above any or all religions. The pluralism that now is present in the world is *an amazing grace*. Pope Paul VI in 1969 in Kampala, Uganda said:

> ***Adaptation of the Christian life in the fields of pastoral, ritual, didactic and spiritual activities are not only possible, it is even favored by the Church. The liturgical renewal is a living example of this. And in this sense you may, and you must, have an African Christianity."***[76]

We need church leaders who are now able to leave the Roman way to the Romans.

---

[75] Roger Haight, "Jesus Symbol of God", Orbis Press, NY p.21
[76] Convocation of the Bishops of African in Kampala, Uganda, July 31, 1969. Acta Apostolicae Sedis 66 (1969): 577.

William L. Forst

Power frequently 'goes-to-the-head' when human made institutions become omnipotent, authoritative, worldwide, and wealthy. These institutions begin to think they are god. When this happens they get into a 'status-quo' frame of life. *'Things are working very well and we just do not need change." or "We have always done it this way."* So much is of this is true today that Herbert Marcuse said *that for an institution to be successful it must make unthinkable the possibility of alternatives.* This is the drive for power, to be self-perpetuating, and the sole guardian of 'our truth'. This stance directly benefits a small minority, those in control, the CEO, pope, president, and a few mid-managers. But the vast majority of people in the institution become upset because their talents, intuition, and creativity are being neglected. A remedy for this is what Thomas Jefferson shaped into the US Constitution the *'party of opposition'*. The responsibility of this party is to bring up different ways of doing things. In this fashion it helps to purify the ideas of the power people. The opposition helps to bring forth a better, more workable, more acceptable manner of doing business. Diversity is accepted, opposites are eliminated, and one learns to love the enemy. Without the opposition party, the power people of the institution sink deeply into a 'status quo' mentality. The institution dies. The theologian Walter Brueggermann[77] says:

---

[77] Walter Brueggmann, "Hopeful Imagination", Fortress Press, Phia. PA 1986 p.26

> *"Resistance, I submit comes from a frightened, crushed imagination that has been robbed of power precisely because of fear. Indeed one can note the abysmal lack of imagination in the formation of policy about either international security or domestics economics. We can think of nothing to do except to do more of the same, which generates only more problems and more fear."*

It seems the Church is presently in this position of rejecting opposition, and diversity of ideas. One of the first things Pope John Paul II did after he was elected was to contain the imagination of Fr. Hans Kung (of Germany) for Kung questioned the idea of 'infallibility'. The church is saying we have no room for new ideas, no room for new questions. No more doubting Thomases. With that in mind there is little chance for a resurrection.

The **Quantum world** says that every segment of creation (even subatomic) is in relationship. The world of spirituality says that love keeps the relationships together. The world of religions have an enormous problem that of accepting the diversity among religions. Religions do not need to be in union regarding dogmas, liturgy, politics or property. Religions needs to be accepting of each other regarding the action of love. Religions need to stop creating these *'insurmountable barriers'* between themselves. It really doesn't matter what religion we believe as long as we are people of love, and as long as we attempt to *"love our neighbor as ourselves."* When we are able to accept the good that the various religions represent, then we will accept the diversity, and then there will be a *"union of opposites."* We will be *'loving the enemy'* as Jesus advocated.

Of recent years there has been a massive rejection of God's diversity in the inner cities of the USA. 100 years ago this diversity consisted of immigrants from various countries of Europe and mostly Roman Catholic and white. There were very few black Catholics integrated into the white catholic community. In most of our cities the diversity was glossed over by making **'National Parishes'** (Polish, German, Irish, etc.) which were an irregularity in canon law. These national parishes did not bring unity. A certain amount of unity only came, in later years, with economic changes. Today the diversity of the inner city has changed substantially to black, brown and yellow, and generally the poor and oppressed. Now, the inner city is made up of Muslims, Buddhist, Protestant, Catholic and other religions. The US Census[78] gives us the appalling statistics of our inner cities. 1 in 5 children live in poverty. 1 in 4 young black men live in prison. Of the children the census shows that 19.2% of all children live below the poverty level. Of this number 36.8% are African Americans, 36.4% are Hispanics, and 15.4% are white. A great number of children in our society do not have competent caretakers or genuine nurturers. This is a national disgrace. But why are the churches moving out of the inner city?

The Catholic Church problem is that it is leaving hundreds of well established and paid for parish plants in the inner city. A more serious problem seems to be the church is not able to accept the present diversity of the inner cities. The Catholic Church (and many

---

[78] U.S. Census Bureau Statistical Abstract of the United States: 1999, 119th ed. (Washington D.C.: U.S. Dept of Commerce 1999) 483

other churches) has moved to the **suburbs**. It has moved because 'our' people (catholic) and the money are now in the suburbs. This has happened in St. Louis in two waves. First, in the 50s-60s, the white Catholics moved from the city to the suburbs (St. Louis County). Now, 80s-90s, they are moving from the St. Louis County across the river to St. Charles county (and Jefferson County). St. Charles County has been building these multimillion-dollar parish plants. Just as General Motors, and now Master Card, built their multimillion-dollar plants in St. Charles County. St. Charles is the place of the new money. It is also the place of the franchise parish. I ask, is this the way Jesus would cure the ills of the inner cites of our land? Is this what the *"option for the poor"* means? Is this the understanding of the beatitudes, *"Blessed are the poor?"*

Years ago during the terrible World War II against the Jews, philosopher Simone Weil, wrote: *"Instead of developing techniques for maximum profit, try to develop those that will give the maximum of freedom: an entirely new approach."* I think this is what Jesus wants us to do. Why are we moving out of the inner city? Today there is even greater diversity in the inner city, greater need, than was present 100 years ago. God's love is unconditional and impartial. So why should the Catholic Church move to the suburbs simply because there are no more of 'our' people in the inner city? Does not God in his unconditional love, love every person of the inner city in all its diversity? It appears the church is following the money.

The rich parishes of the suburbs are building multimillion dollar plants, that consist of very expensive property, beautiful schools with many teachers, and a lavish recreational set up (gymnasium and playing fields), with large (1500-2000 seating) beautiful cathedrals, and presently these parishes are building smaller chapels for wedding, funerals etc. A recent article in the Monitor[79] indicates the Catholic Church in American is easily the **richest in the world.** The article indicates that the church receives more than $13 billion in contributions annually which amounts to $253 million a week. Why can't these rich parishes share their wealth with the inner city? Isn't that what Jesus would do, WWJD? Are not the readings for 26th Sunday of the year (Amos 6:1-7 and Lk. 16:19-31) both readings telling us that we cannot be complacent about the poor? The not named 'rich man' was being complacent; he paid no attention to Lazarus. The rich man passed Lazarus each day, but apparently did not know or realize that Lazarus existed. He was so involved in living in the suburbs. What does **'love of neighbor'** mean other than noticing the poor and taking some action to make things better for the poor? Should we be concerned about what religion the poor people profess?

Even the priest personnel are taken away from the inner city and put where the money is. Isn't the Catholic Church of USA buying into what Simone Weil calls the *'techniques for maximum profit'*, and being unmindful of the inner city people? Should not the church be vitally interested in the outcasts of our society (Mt 25:30-46) and trying to develop these folks to have *'maximum freedom'*,

---

[79] Mark Clayton, Christina Science Monitor, "Scandals will dent, not bankrupt, dioceses." March 28, 2002 p. 3

health care, education, housing, and to have safe neighborhoods? I think God is delighted with the diversity of religions we have in the world, and in our inner cities, all attempting to enable people to love one another. If we cannot accept this diversity that exists in the inner city, are we able to be a church with a spiritual mission?

This unwillingness to accept the diversity in our inner cities comes from our inability to accept diversity among religions. This is negatively expressed in Northern Ireland, Bosnia, Palestine/Israel, Iraq and during World War II. **Is this not the problem of the bombing of the World Trade Center?** The unwillingness of religions to accept one another is the basic cause of modern war. The religious leaders are not accepting their responsibility before God. Theologians of all religions are calling the leaders of religions to dialogue. This dialogue must proceed with mutual understanding, mutual appreciation one for the other. Accepting the beautiful diversity in religions, and be willing to learn of what is the truth in other religions. If a religion is not open to learning, then there can be no dialogue. Fr. Roger Haight[80] writes,

> *'It is difficult to see how the recognition of God at work in other religious mediations in any way undermines the radically affirming sense of being addressed by God and united to God through Jesus.'*

Sandra N. Schneiders writes about John's 4th gospel. One point she makes is that God comes to the disciples directly and not

---

[80] US Census Bureau Ibid p. 423

necessarily through the authority of a church institution. This is shown so beautifully in the story of the blind man (Jn 9:1-41). The blind man came to believe that Jesus was the Messiah (9:38) even after he was thrown out of the church institution (synagogue) (9:22). This church (many today) believes that it has direct contact with God and there was no other way. Jesus was showing that the institution (all churches) does not have control over our access to God. Schneiders makes a brilliant point in this matter of accepting diversity;

> *"Increasingly Christians are coming to realize that their faith in Jesus as 'unique', 'definitive,' 'absolute' revelation of God need not mean 'only' and must allow for the possibility and indeed the actuality of other saving manifestations of God in other religious traditions. This is the central challenge of an adequate theology of religions, which most theologians agree is still in the future. No matter how it is eventually formulated, it must take account of two seemingly incompatible but necessary facts: on the one hand, one cannot really believe in a 'relative' God; on the other hand, one cannot believe in a God who is not available to all people."*[81]

Thomas Friedman[82], in reference to the Taliban of Afghanistan, wrote an editorial, **"Religious Totalitarianism"** or **"God can hear many voices."** He mentions that the three faiths coming

---

[81] Sandra M. Schneiders, "Written That You May Believe", Crossroads Pub., NY, 1999p. 88-89. She gives new and very insightful understanding of the 4th gospel.
[82] Tomas Friedman. "St. Louis Post-Dispatch", copyrighted from New York Times, November 29, 2001, p. c17

from Abraham, Judaism, Christianity, and Islam, all have had a tendency to regard themselves as having an exclusive and lawful relationship with God. They bought into *"Religious Totalitarianism."* This is presently bin Ladenism. Our war is against this ideology of *"Religious Totalitarianism."* Peace will come when all religions teach that, *"God can hear many voices."*

It is absolutely important that the world religions respect the diverse faiths in which God mediates with his people here on earth. It was long ago that Peter learned from Cornelius, *"that God shows no partiality"* (Acts 10:34). How long will it take the religions of today to believe that God is a God with unconditional love for all people, for all religions, all races, and all sexes?

Unity as uniqueness

I feel, more strongly than ever, the need of freeing our religion from everything about it that is specifically Mediterranean.
Teilhard de Chardin

Possibly one of the greatest necessities of acquiring unity among human beings is the recognition of the dignity of the human being, also our uniqueness in the eyes of God. We fulfill our spiritual needs through our individual human characteristics. Each human being yearns to be accepted in our individuality and uniqueness. This begins at birth and continues until death. I heard on the radio (August 1998) a child psychologist taking about young children entering school for the first time. She said that in order that the many fears might be lessened, the child needs to be welcomed and then assured that their uniqueness will be respected.

Baptism ritual of the Christian church is beautifully unique, and it respects all people as unique who submit themselves to this ritual. For it does not matter if you are, 'male-female, slave-free, Jew-Gentile,' all are baptized in the same fashion, and all are accepted as equals, and yet all are very different and unique. The great feast of Pentecost is all about the unique persons being accepted in the church, **"*people from around the world*"** received the Spirit of God. People from different religions, different cultures, different languages and God is with them.

The four gospels of the New Testament are each very unique. For each gospel was born out of different and diverse community. From the beginning the church built itself into nine unique rites: Latin, Roman or Western (this is ours), Byzantine, Armenian, Chaldean, **Coptic**, Ethiopian, Malabar, Maronite and Syrian. A rite expresses a unique way of prayer, belief, life, and culture. These rites were formed from the bottom-up that is they developed from the people that the church served. The church spread to Alexandria, Egypt, and then to Nubia (Sudan) and Ethiopia, and they developed a very distinctive rite called the Coptic rite.[83] this rite prevails to this day. The early church enjoyed and celebrated this diversity. However within a few hundred years these rituals of uniqueness

---

[83] "The Modern Catholic Encyclopedia", (Michael Glazier, Liturgical Press, Collegeville, MN, 1994) Art. "Easter Catholic Churches" p. 257-261

became a power-struggle, between the east and the west. Dirty politics entered the church. This came to a head in 1054 when the eastern Patriarch excommunicated the western Pope, and vice versa. Pope Paul VI and the Patriarch of the East finally lifted these excommunications in 1965.

Today the uniqueness is not only the East and West; it is the North and South. In fact we are told that by the year 2015 the South will dominate the Church in USA, and it will no longer be under the influence of Europe (North). Pablo Richard[84] of Costa Rica distinguishes two extremes of Church models. One he calls the **'church-society'**, which is a church structured by hierarchy of powers and a rigid caste system (north). The other is **'church-community'** (south), which is structured around small communities. In the south the Bishops are not at the summit of power, but in the center of a community of believers. Vatican II has asked the Church to inculterate itself (adapt the church to a culture, not a culture to the church) into the unique societies of Africa and **South America**. With the age of Colonization (1400-1700) there was little if any incultration of the Church. The Church adapted the American Indian culture (they were called savages - they had no culture) to the European Church culture, rather than the adapting the Church to the Indian Culture. Much the same was done in Africa and South America. The Church is paying a very high price for this today. Today the Church is attempting to inculturate itself into the very unique cultures around

---

[84] Gary MacEoin, ed., "The Papacy and the People of God", (Orbis Books, Maryknoll, N.Y., 1998) Article by Pablo Richard p. 131-143

the world, the south and east. This is proving to be a tremendous difficulty, yet it has to be done if the Church is to become a global institution. In all of this inculteration we have the necessity of working with the Vatican II principal ideas of collegiality and subsidiarity.

In 1960 the priests of our diocese (Jefferson City) were offered a chance to volunteer for service in Peru, South America. I volunteered and felt good that my uniqueness was being accepted. I was not able to fulfill my pledge to Peru until 1974. At this time, I felt uniquely prepared for I had taught history in our Minor Seminary for six years, also experienced the openness that came out of Vatican II Council, and my adventures in the **Social Concern** (Catholic Charities) for four years. All of this prepared me for this unique mission and chance of a lifetime. Why would some priests volunteer for this mission and others not? Because of our uniqueness. We looked upon church differently; our understanding of the purpose of the church was different. We saw the poverty of the people of Peru in a distinct fashion. This was a very unique situation in the Church, and it needed people who were in touch with and who accepted their own uniqueness.

After language school, I was sent to the Parish of **Nasca, Peru.** I found out quickly, that before I could give anything to the people of Peru, I had to learn a great deal about the Peruvian People, their unique understanding of faith, unique family structure, unique government etc. Everything was different. I learned to accept, and to appreciate the unique manner in which the Peruvian people lived. I experienced the deep faith and hope of the People of God. I was no longer attempting to change the People of Peru, but I was working feverishly to change myself. This is very difficult for me to accept my own uniqueness, but even more difficult for me to accept the uniqueness of other people. But only in accepting this uniqueness will we ever find unity. The Peruvian people helped me to accept the amazing diversity and unity of the People of God around the world.

I realize that in all of this there is a living contradiction for the church. For how does one accept uniqueness and individuality on the one hand, and community and plurality on the other hand. Yet we have to find a way to accept both individuality and community. Individual human beings have to have their uniqueness recognized if their dignity is to be realized. On the other hand, human beings are social animals and have a fundamental need for community. There has to be a way of accepting diversity and still not driving each individual into a person they are not. Scripture is clear on this matter. Paul's writings speak of the unique ways of the disciples: (Rom 12:6-8 & I Cor12: 5-29) speaks of different gifts, prophecy, ministry, teaching, exhortation, generosity, diligence, administration, variety of tongues, and mercy. I Cor: 12:4 **"There are different kinds of spiritual gifts but the same Sprit"**. Community comes only when the uniqueness of each is recognized and celebrated.

William L. Forst

Dr. Rachel N. Remen[85] tells many inspiring stories about her many patients, she says in part,

> **"after all these years of listening it seems to me that the essential quality of the human soul is uniqueness. Each of us is one of a kind. None of us has existed in the history of the human race before."** Remen talks about a CEO who is recovering from cancer, he said, **"I am shocked to have discovered this morning that I am the only me there is."**

Months later this man is looking at life and people around him in a very different manner. He now looks with respect and seeing the dignity of people he meets. Remen mentions, *"What this man used to perceive as differences to be judged and possibly dismissed he now sees as uniqueness to be appreciated and understood."* My life as a priest has grown in similar fashion. The education and training I have had in the many years of seminary and priesthood, I find it very easy to judge those who are not of my belief, and not to see the uniqueness of the other to be appreciated and understood.

The modern church is finding it difficult recognizing the uniqueness of the People of God. Uniqueness is the same as diversity to the church. But diversity is what we have made ourselves and uniqueness is what God has made us.

---

[85] Rachel Naomi Remen, M.D. "Kitchen table Wisdom", Riverhead Books, NY p.285

Spirituality as Listening Brings Unity

Rabbi Herschel defines sin as
'The Human's refusal to become who we are'

Listening is one of the most important actions that a servant leader performs. Listening expresses trust. Aristotle taught dialogue, one cannot dialogue unless one learns the art of deep listening. We cannot know 'who we are' without listening to God and others in prayer, and without dialoguing with God and others. When a leader listens the leader indicates that he/she is able to learn from the other. When there is true listening, there will be trust, and spirituality will be developed, unity will flow.

How really do we listen? Judging from Jesus, listening is very difficult. Jesus was frustrated often, once he said to his disciples *"You have ears to hear, but you can not hear* (Mk 8:18)." The many times Jesus seemed to be 'fit to be tied' at the inability of his disciples to understand what he was saying. Jesus said, *"You of little faith"(*Mt 16: 8-10), and you *"hear and listen but do not understand"* (Mk 4:12-13). How much he wanted his disciples to deeply listen to what he was saying. But what is deep listening?

Stephen Carter[86] makes a very necessary principal in listening, *"Civility requires that we listen to others with knowledge of the possibility that they are right and we are wrong."* It says, the listener

---

[86] Stephen Carter, "Civility", (Basic Books, New York, N.Y. 1998) ps 132-147.

William L. Forst

is fallible, makes mistakes of judgment, and frequently is wrong. When the listener gets this notion across, there will be trust. This is true if you happen to be the CEO of General Motors, a bishop, president or pastor. No human being is infallible, and we are to listen as though we might be wrong and the other party might well be right, or that we might learn something.

An autocratic, domineering institution, or person, implies that it has nothing to listen to, or nothing to learn. The institution that does not listen, forfeits faith, confidence, and trust. This is one of the underlying truths to the statement that, *"power corrupts and absolute power corrupts absolutely"*. The church has always had its problems in listening to prophets. Jeremiah and Isaiah of the Hebrew scriptures where not listened to. Instead of listening to Galileo, in the 1500s, with the possibility the Church was wrong, the Church excommunicated the scientist. The same was done to Martin Luther and the Reformers. Autocratic business and government institutions do the same in trying to eliminate the 'whistle -blowers.'

Frs. Teilhard de Chardan, Matthew Fox, and Tissa Balasuriya all came up with a different expressions of Original Sin. Chardin,[87] without being given a chance to explain, was put under strict orders to change his views, and then he was sent to China. Fox and **Balasuriya**

---

[87] Ursula King, "Spirit of Fire", (Orbis Books, N.Y. 1998) ps. 106-109 In part Teilhard said, "It is no exaggeration to say that, in the form in which it is still commonly presented today, original sin is at the moment one of the chief obstacles that stand in the way of the intensive and extensive progress of Christian thought". He came upon this idea from the science of Paleontology.

If Aristotle Ran the Catholic Church

faired about the same. Except that in Fr. Tissa Balasuriya's case the Vatican dropped its judgment against him. Could it be the Curia was wrong and did not listen? This is one of the difficulties with people and institutions that are domineering and autocratic, and claim that they make no mistakes. They also turn out to be poor listeners.

I like the creation story told around Eve. Adam obviously was going nowhere without a woman. He soon understood that there was no passion or spirit with the many beautiful animals all around him, nor did he get much inspiration from beautiful plants, trees or the environment in which he lived. God appointed him as CEO of the world of creation. He was given the task to control this magnificent mess, to bring order out of chaos. Adam was not up to the job and was at the point of losing his high position. When God began to listen to Adam and hear his difficulties. God then constructed a woman and when Adam took a look at the woman he said, **"WOW"**, **"This at last is bone of my bones and flesh of my flesh; she shall be called Woman, because she was taken out of Man** [Gen 2:23]**."** Lord you really hit the nail on the head this time. You listened deeply to my concerns and difficulties. You provided a most wonderful solution. Indeed you are God.

Later **Adam** would indicate that the woman gives him passion to enjoy creation; her passion helps him to make relationships. With her passion Adam is able to listen to creation, she gives him spirit so that both can dance and play. Above all the woman gives Adam the capacity to share in new life. With this new life both can bring God's creation to its fulfillment. Adam quickly found out that he was barren, impotent, and childless without woman. Without women there would be no new beginnings or resurrections. Adam was so pleased that God listened to him. He was very pleased that women were made equal to man.

I see the present challenge to the Roman Church today as, **"is the church able and willing to listen deeply to women?"** Are women essential to the church? Can the Church function without women? Is the church impotent (as Adam was) without women? Can women be priests? The answers will be found when the Church brings itself to listen to women and to all the people of the world. There is no spirituality without listening.

Spirituality is Friendship

**No longer do I call you servants,
for the servant does not know what his master is doing;
but I have called you friends; for all that I have heard
from my Father I have made known to you.** John 15:15

One of the most amazing acts of leadership that Jesus performed is washing the feet of his disciples (Jn 13: 4-15). This is mentioned only in John's gospel. Sr. Sandra Schneiders,[88] a scripture scholar, affords an enlivening understanding of this story. There is no leader in the world, religious or otherwise, who has advocated this sort of self-humiliation. It is almost as scandalizing as the crucifixion.

---

[88] Sandra M. Schneiders, "Written That You May Believe", Crossroads Pub. Co. NY, 1999

It also occupies a very central part of John's gospel - the beginning of the Eucharist before his death. It no doubt shocked his disciples as it obviously upset Peter (v.8). Jesus was not sure that his disciples would accept this expression of leadership for after he washed their feet Jesus said, *"Do you understand what I have done to you? (*v.12)."* Then Jesus said that <u>you need to do this to one another.</u> This 'foot washing' fits in so well with the other leadership traits that Jesus mentioned: taking the last place, don't accept titles of honor, don't wear clothes that set one off from the people, let your leadership (and spirituality) be surrounded with humility and patience. Do not pattern your leadership or spirituality after the rulers of the day.

Mutuality and **equality** are necessary subjects in friendship spirituality. There is no place for domination, manipulation, or subordination. There is no room for slavery in friendship spirituality. Friendship leadership will be most effective because trust will be present. Where there is domination and slavery there is no trust. Jesus so beautifully said, *"No longer do I call you servants (slaves)—but I call you friends."* This is a radical change in leadership for Jesus' time as well as our own time. Jesus knew very well who he was as a leader, and the exalted position he had as Son of God, for he said: *"You call me Teacher and Lord; and you are right, for so I am* (v.13)." But knowing this Jesus stated firmly that humility, service, and love is what he wants to see in all his disciples especially the leaders. Jesus wants his disciples to be friends.

It is exciting to realize that Aristotle has three types of friendship.[89] The First is **Pleasure** friendship, which arises from a sensual pleasure that the friends mutually give to one another. The Second is **Utility** friendship because of some usefulness of one to another. Such as Employer to employee. The Third is **Perfected** friendship. This is the type of friendship Aristotle deems necessary for leaders in the polis (city). One wants what is good for the friend for the friend's sake. It recognizes the qualities of the friend. It honors and celebrates these qualities. **Aristotle says this friendship is between equals**. I suspect Jesus was aware of these forms of friendship from Aristotle's teaching. For Jesus is saying almost the same as Aristotle, *"No longer are you called slaves, but friends, for I have great trust in you, and I can share everything that I am with you."* Sr. Sandra M. Schneiders[90] helps us to understand the radical call for spirituality and service that 'washing the feet' invokes. She lines up three types or models of service:

1. *Must Do* service. Freedom is not involved in this service, e.g. Father & Mother toward son or daughter, a slave to their owner, a pastor to his bishop, employee to the boss or even a person attending Mass or performing a religious activity because of 'obligation' (they will go to hell if they don't perform). We are not saying right or wrong here, but just the way it is done. This 'must do' service carries

---

[89] Daniel N. Robinson, "The Great Ideas of Philosophy", Georgetown University, The Teaching Company, Tape 13
[90] Sandra M. Schneiders, "Written That You may Believe", Crossroads Pub. Co. NY, 1999. p. 166-174. Sr. Schnieders has a very readable and lucid understanding of John's story of the 'Food Washing'.

with it a condition of inequality. This 'must do' service is able to be structured into a loving situation. However, most of the time, the structure becomes one of dominance frequently becoming exploitative and even oppressive. Jesus showed great inner freedom in acting against this type of leadership exhibited by Pilat (Jn. 19:10-11)

2. *Does freely* service. This service is given out of a natural attraction to one another, e.g. Mother or Father toward a child, a psychiatrist to a client, pastor to his 'sheep',

3. *Friendship* service. This relationship is based upon equals. Domination cannot exist between friends. True Christian friendship in human relationships must be based on equality. This is the ideal for marriage; it is possible in a relationship between a boss and employee, between pastor and flock, and between bishop and pope. We will have here the **'Discipleship of equals'**, as Elizabeth S. Fiorenza advocates. Jesus also advocates this type of relationship with his disciples (Jn 15:15). He was speaking to his disciples shortly after he washed their feet. He said, *"No longer do I call you servants... I now call you friends."*

Liturgically, in Catholic Church, leaders perform this very meaningful act of *'washing the feet of the disciples'* only once a year (and this is not mandatory) on Holy Thursday. There are some people who think this 'foot washing' should be a necessary part of the liturgy - especially for the leaders. It immediately brings to our mind the leadership that Jesus advocated. Some say the washing of the feet should be performed each time (certainly on Sundays) the Mass is celebrated. Some consider it almost as important as receiving Communion.

This spirituality of friendship is presently solely desired and needed within the leadership of the church. Especially with the present church scandal (2002) many are saying it is a leadership defect. Our leaders are not willing to 'wash the feet' of those they serve. The absence of friendship in leadership is a dominant reason that so few people desire to be priests.

Spirituality Makes the Servant Leader

"He/She who is the greatest among you shall be your servant"
Mt: 23; 11

In the last 50 years we have been exposed to many scandals regarding our clergy. This has become possible because of the openness and freedom of our society enhanced by the high tech communications. However these scandals are not something new. The People of God are asking for the first time, **"Are our Servant Leaders imitating the person of Jesus?"** We do **not** need dominant leaders, or bosses, or know-it-all dictators, but we need leaders who respect the People of God. We need leaders who are willing to *'wash the feet'* of the People of God as Jesus did. We need leaders who do not choose the first place, leaders who do not separate themselves from the people by titles or power clothes (crowns, miters) or pageantry. To indicate that there was a strong thrust to do this very thing during Vatican II Council, I quote from my brother Marion who was present at the council. He wrote the following during the council:

> *"Every time I attend Papal ceremonies at St. Peter's I have the feeling that if ever I should lose my faith (may God prevent) it would be because of these ceremonies. Really, not the Papal ceremonies or the Pope, but the pageantry that goes with it. For me the problem is that I cannot conceive of all this 'spectaculum' being of one whit's value to the Church in either presenting Christ or Christ's message to the world. It seems just so much comic-opera stuff that in today's world is out of place for the Church. To me it seems that the Church is living in the past and trying to reclaim the glory of the days when the Popes were also kings."*[91]

What is sorely needed presently is a drastic change in the clergy culture. I do believe that with the addition of women in the priesthood, the present clergy culture will change radically. People are seeking a religion that has leaders who are free to open themselves up to the Spirit of God. We don't need a co-dependent clergy who can neither think for themselves, nor freely follow God's Spirit.

The spirituality of a servant leader is nurtured by a loving relationship with the sheep, "He **knows his sheep and they know him"**. The Hebrew word for 'know' indicates a very intimate, personal, and loving relationship. The commitment made in this relationship is equal to the marriage commitment. The spirituality of the servant leader is based upon a '***Power-with***' those who are led. It is based upon equality - that all people are created to God's Image.

---

[91] Marion F. Forst, "Daily Journal of Vatican II", Forest of Peace Pub. 2000 p.67

The spirituality of servant leaders drives the leaders to operate in freedom, and permits freedom to their charges. This servant leader respects the dignity of human beings as they respect his/her dignity as leader.

The spirituality of a dominating, autocratic leader is based upon *'power-over'* their charges. This leader is an entirely different type than Jesus talked about. This type of leader denies not only the freedom of the led but also their own freedom. Their spiritually is based upon their ego, their political power, at times their military or coercive power, and manipulation that generates fear. These leaders do not recognize the dignity of the individual. With the advent of high tech communications, controlling leaders may control vast number of people and resources. But there is no personal commitment; they are not able to 'know' their people. It is almost impossible for them to '***wash the feet***' of their people. This is happening in large parishes of 10,000 to 20,000 people, as well in large dioceses and gigantic corporations.

Servant leadership leads to peace, while controlling leadership leads to resistance. Even General Motors and many other large business organizations and corporations have learned over the years that a controlling and domineering leadership leads to less productivity and that means less for the share holder. This type of leadership is rejected in the end. It is not the way to make money.

If Aristotle Ran the Catholic Church

Servant Leader Evokes Community

"The ability to empower is what makes great leadership a servanthood: It awakens the slumbering power in the souls of others."
Bishop Bennett Sims

Community is so important and necessary that we almost take it for granted. Community is ever present in the scriptures, and written about often in the Vatican II documents. I don't think one can acquire spirituality without community. No 'man' is an island. Isn't community the very purpose of God creating Adam and Eve? The scriptures were formed out of a community. We as Christians are people who have been developed out of a community.

On January 6, 2001 Pope John Paul II issued his letter "Novo Millennio Uneunte" (At the beginning of the New Millennium).[92] The Pope says that communion *"embodies and reveals the very essence of the mystery of the church."* He says,

> *"In accordance with the Second Vatican Council's major directives, will serve to ensure and <u>safeguard communion</u>. How can we forget in the first place those specific services to communion that are the Petrine ministry and, closely related to it, <u>episcopal collegiality</u>?".* He talks about the *"<u>structures of participation</u> envisaged by canon law, such as the council of priests and the pastoral council, must be ever more highly valued......The theology and spirituality of communion encourage a <u>fruitful dialogue</u>*

---

[92] Francis A. Sullivan S.J. "The Magisterium in the New Millennium", America Mag. August 27-September 3, 2001 p.12

between pastors and faithful: "The Pope indicates that the '***structures of participation***' must involve *"fruitful dialogue"* and *"open to discussion,"* and this helps to form community. Yet what seems to be happening is that the Pope is '***talking the talk***', and the Curia is an obstacle to permitting the church to '***walk the walk***'. The Curia has all but shut off dialogue and discussion on important issues which involve Roman Catholic ***'structures of participation'*** for today's community

The following couple of paragraphs are supported by a pamphlet, "Jesus and Community", written by Fr. Roger Karban.[93] The early Christian community celebrated the resurrection of Jesus. The presence of Jesus was very real in the members of the community. When community met they shared in a meal of the Body and Blood of Jesus. Today, as we drink, eat, and celebrate (the Mass) we commit ourselves to be the 'real presence' of Jesus in our everyday life. This is real purpose of the Mass, a loving, living community on the go, giving the disciples the courage and bravery to be **Jesus real presence**, to be his feet, his arms, his mouth in the local community.

There are those today who put great emphasis upon the tabernacle. Some say doing '***Perpetual adioration***' is making the Eucharist too individualistic, and evading the presence of Jesus in the suffering community. A friend of mine once said about 'perpetual adoration', ***"It is wonderful for people to spend an hour in adoration of the Blessed Sacrament at 3am in the morning, but the next hour***

---

[93] Roger Karban, "Jesus and Community", Victorious Missionaries, Belleville, IL. It is only 20 pages and very readable. I hope you all read this marvelous booklet.

(4-5am) should be spent with the homeless in our inner cities." Then they will be able to be Jesus' real presence, and be committed to the work of the beatitudes. Fr. Karl Rahner held the opinion

> *"that Jesus' earliest followers believed Jesus was no longer present in any wine or bread remaining after the Eucharist was finished, unless the elements were set aside to be taken to those (sick) unable to be present."*[94]

The earliest Christians discovered the risen Jesus in their community. Certainly that is what the Emmaus story is about in Luke 24 13-35. Mr. & Mrs. Clophas recognized the risen Jesus as they sat down to meal. *"Were not our hearts burning"* and then he vanished from their sight.

Sr. Sandra Schneiders [95] writes of the intimate character of the community as it exists in John's gospel. Jesus' one command was *"Everyone will know you are my disciples, if you have love for one another (Jn 13:35)."*

Schneiders says in part:

> *"The fourth Gospel shows little interest in the institutional aspects of 'Church', a word we do not find in this Gospel. As already mentioned, office and titles are not significant in this community. On the contrary, the only preferential status is closeness to Jesus, and that is equally open to men and women, Samaritans, Gentiles, and Jews.*

---

[94] Ibid p.13
[95] Sandra M. Schneiders, "Written that you May Believe" Crossroads Pub. NY, 1999

This seems to have been a thoroughly egalitarian community." [96]

Bishop Bennett J. Sims[97] gives us many ideas and images of what a servant leader might be. One great factor of a Servant leader is to empower people to do their best to respond to the Spirit of God. When this is done the whole community grows. This is the power of Jesus over his disciples and apostles. The Twelve were not religious professionals of the Jewish Church, but men picked off the street. They no doubt were ignorant, and probably rather uncouth, and uneducated, but Jesus saw their deep faith. Jesus brought out the best in his disciples. Jesus empowered them. With most of his cures Jesus said, **"Your faith *(*not the faith of Jesus*)* has made you well."** The person cured must have been greatly energized by this. Jesus recognized that all people, poor, crippled, pagans, homosexuals, Samaritans all had deep faith. Jesus energized the faith of people he met. This empowered faith is what brings life into a community.

The spirituality of Servant leaders drives them to collegial or collaborative associations. It is here that they become **"disciples of equals"** as Jesus indicated. There is not only a *power-with* the people, but also a true feeling of shared vision. In an atmosphere of freedom there is the liberty to tell the truth. There is feeling of real

---

[96] Ibid p. 60
[97] Bennett J. Sims; "Servanthood", (Cowley Publications, Boston, MA. 1997) ps.28-41. The whole book is a treasure in attempting to understand what Jesus means by a Servant Leader. Bishop Sims comes from the Anglican tradition.

belonging of having ownership. All of this ensures community. I think it is safe to say that a servant leader is truly the copy of Jesus.

Elizabeth Dominguez,[98] from the Philippines, interprets Genesis 1:26, *"To be in the image of God is to be in community. It is not simply a man or a woman who can reflect God, but it is the community in relationship."* In real community all people are servant leaders to one another. This community is characterized by **"interdependence, harmony, and mutual growth."** However when power is monopolized, as in patriarchy or dictatorship, mutuality, harmony, and interdependence are destroyed. Where there is no mutual relationship there is no human experience of God.[99] This is a reflection of Asian women theologians.

I like what Larry Rassmussen[100] writes about the Christian character of leadership. He labels the leadership style as '**community democracy**', which we certainly see in the Council of Jerusalem of the Acts of Apostles. Rassmussen states that community democracy depends upon,

"Shifting leadership, high levels of member participation, the capacity of its organizers and troublemaker

---

[98] Chung Hyun Kyung, "Struggle to be the Sun Again", Orbis Books, Maryknoll, NY. 1990, p. 48. Chung gives a beautiful description of community among Christian women in Asia.

[99] ibid p. 49

[100] Larry Rasmussen, "Shapin Communities," Ed Dorothy C. Bass (San Francisco: Jossey-Bass, 1997), 121.Also from Ann Pederson's great book, "God, Creation, and all that Jazz", Chalice Press, St. Louis, MO. 2001, p. 75.

to see through the dominant ways of doing things, and a collective ability to offer alternatives."

None of the above is available in the Catholic Church today; we have leaders that stay in for life, the members have little if any ability to effectively participate, the prophets are spurned, there are no alternatives available. There is very little Servant Leadership.

Form the Pope's letter we are to realize that community **"embodies and reveals the very essence of the mystery of the church."** Community is all about relationships among people. These relationships are conducted in freedom, a freedom to respond to God's Spirit. It is in this community that one seeks the Glory of God and is open to the totally unexpected that God brings. It is in this community where God is allowed to be God. A servant leader is needed today to lead this community. A servant leader can bring about a revolution.

Spirituality is Our Work

"Fundamentally, we work to create, and only incidentally do we work to eat."
Willis Harman and John Hormann

Many philosophers talk about the importance of the work that we do. Many philosophers say that we are to exploit one's gifts of imagination and creativity in our work. In fact the first book of the Bible states the necessity, beauty, and creativity of our work (Genesis

1 26- 31). Our work is the guardianship we have over God's creation. Our work involves the humans created to God's image, the sea and it's life, the forests and it's beauty, and all the living creatures of the earth. For God '*saw all he had made, and indeed it was very good*.' Our spirituality is wrapped around this work that keeps our spirit alive.

We live in a society that views work as a means to make money. **Money is the bottom line.** Our culture best values work when you make a good deal of money, and worse when we make minimum wage. People today are judged as to their 'goodness' by the amount of money they make. If you happen to be rich there is less a chance that you will land in prison. If you are poor or if you are a black male between 16 and 25 years of age, there is a 25% chance you will land in prison. It is this group that has high unemployment or under-employment - they have no money. But the work God intends all of us to do, has very little to do with money. God knows that we need money to keep body and soul together. But money is not the end all of our work.

The work we do is very ritualized. We go to bed in the evening so as to give us enough sleep, so as to work fully alive. We dress properly, eat sufficiently, and leave our home in sufficient time to arrive at work at the proper time. We are then present at our work ready to use our creative, and imaginative gifts to exercise guardianship over the little responsibility of God's creation that has been given to us. There are many rituals that we go through to do our work. Work occupies our prime time.

Fr. Matthew Fox[101] speaks of **work as a sacrament**, indeed it has all the qualifications for a sacrament. It is at work where we confront the Body of Christ. It is at work that we build the Church, the People of God. It is at work that we can heal others and be healed by ourselves. Fox indicates, at some length, that all work needs reinventing. Fox indicates an entire environmental revolution is needed in farming, politics, education, sexuality, health care, psychology, art, economics, business, science and technology.[102]

During the Gulf War, in the early 1990s, I questioned a friend who worked at McDonald-Douglas Co. I asked him, *'Do you accept any responsibility for making the guidance systems that direct the bombs that kill innocent Iraqi people?'* After some time of thought he simply said, *'No, that belongs to the President Bush who initiated the war.'* The thought occurred to me this man carries no moral responsibility for his work, he is just doing his 'job'; he is working for the Friday check. He is not getting paid to think, to make decisions, even to act morally.

This McDonald-Douglas man does not ask these work questions: What are the moral consequences of my work? Who is profiting from my work? How are the poor being helped by my work? Are the rich getting richer and the poor poorer by my work?

---

[101] Matthew Fox, "The Reinvention of Work" Harper, San Francisco, 1994 p.296-308.
[102] Ibid Fox.

Do I have any moral responsibility in my work? Albert Einstein is said to have remarked that almost all scientist are dependent on economics - or the Friday check. And then he was supposed to have said that there are very few scientists who posses a sense of social or moral responsibility. On the other hand, J. Robert Oppenheimer is said to have remarked upon the detonation of the atomic bomb, *'Now we have known evil'*. With that he announced a new era of science, and era of interconnection, and of moral responsibility. I truly believe this is presently going on from reading books by Rupert Sheldrake and Jan G. Babour.[103]

It seems that the Catholic Church, in USA, the richest county in the world is beset with materialism, commercialism, and greed. The Pastors of all religions must deal with the question each day *how can we keep values of Jesus' beatitudes and also have an up to date, parish? How can the Church be counter culture*? This is our work. This is the work of leadership.

The song of servant leadership brings hope to the church

---

[103] Rupert Sheldrake & Matthre Fox, "Natural Grace', Doubleday, NY, 1997; Jan G. Barbour, "When Science Meets Religion", Harper, San Francisco, 2000. And there are many more.

Conclusion

"God is the improviser of the world, with tender patience, composing it with her vision of truth, beauty, and goodness."
Alfred North Whitehead

The title given to the book **"If Aristotle Ran the Catholic Church"** is humorous, as is the title of many books, e.g. "If Aristotle Ran General Motors'. However this book has its very serious side. I have tried to bring an answer to an age old question for the Church, **"What does it mean the be a Servant Leader in the Church?"** And what style of leadership is appropriate for USA in 2003? Leadership bears amazing responsibility in all institutions, especially hierarchic and beaucratric types. If the leadership is honest and truthful in performing its duties it will have the **trust** of the people. Presently, I believe, that, in the United States, the Bishops are not receiving the trust they need to lead.

In answering this question the modern church has the responsibility of doing a balancing act between the creative, the new, the experiential with the traditional and the status quo mentality. It seems that the status quo has full power today. 500 years ago the church was in the same situation with Martin Luther. He was the new and creative and the church took the safe position of the status quo. Luther went back to the scriptures and found a leadership that was fallible, the leaders were equal with the people, the leaders were in touch with the people - he called it the 'Priesthood of the people'. The Catholic Church would not listen to Luther - he was a heretic and the church was ready to kill him. Thank God the church does not have that kind of power today. However there are those in today's leadership who want to restore the church back to Luther's time and the Council of Trent, or certainly back to the time before Vatican II. This council restored the use of Luther's phrase, "Priesthood of the People", and we now use it in our Baptismal ritual.

Ann Peterson in her marvelous book, **'God, Creation, and all that Jazz'**[104] gives us some wonderful insights into this question. She compares church leadership to 2 models of music - orchestration and improvisation. Musically both styles are acceptable and proper but very different in the playing of music. We are not talking about good or evil, right or wrong, heresy or orthodox - but the style of leadership that is needed today - 2003. The church is global (not only European) and needs a leadership that is tuned into the world. In short it needs a catholic (universal) leadership.

Peterson develops two styles of leadership:

1. **Orchestration** depends upon a well thought out plan - score. This plan will not take place unless there is order and cooperation, which must lead to a blending of the great number of diverse instruments. The conductor who holds almost infallible authority over the orchestra enforces the order and cooperation.

---

[104] Ann Peterson, "God, Creation, and all that Jazz", Chalice Press, St. Louis MO.2001

William L. Forst

When the blending happens then we hear beautiful music. Max Roach says the following:

> *"In European classical music the two most important people are the composer and conductor. They are like king and queen. In a sense, the conductor is also the military official who's there to see that the wishes of the masters - the composers - are adhered to, and as a musician your job may depend on how you conform to the conductor's interpretation of the composer's wishes."*[105]

This is a picture of European Classical theology of the western Catholic Church today. God is creator and controls all. We are God's creatures and we are created as God's Image. God is the composer of the score and conductor of the orchestra. We, as God's creatures, are to follow his infallible plan. We are not to compose, or to co-create. We are not to conduct, but only obey.

2. **Improvisation** emphasizes the necessity of relationship, or the relationship of the individual to the group. Each musician expresses their own unique skill with their instrument, while the group gives the needed support. Ann Peterson comes to our assistance:

> *"It is not the monologue of one composer or conductor using his musicians to realize his vision of the master plan... The leader does not dominate the group, insisting it be played his or her way. The composition is built along the way; it becomes a project that is creative, cooperative. In a world where there isn't one universal*

---

[105] Ibid, p. 25

voice, or one song, the image of blues and jazz offers an alternative way of creating and playing the compositions of God. Our role is that of the created co-creator." [106]

I believe that music is a sure way of involving the heart, for we know the power and force of the song put to music. What tremendous influence has the song **"We Shall Overcome'** been in the Black civil rights movement.

Music has the ability of entering the heart of people. Jesus frequently indicated that **'I want to change your heart'**. The changed heart will then change the intellect. Today the church seems to move on the intellect in order that it may operate infallibly. Or we may say the opposite that the church moves infallibly in order to assert the intellect and reason. We know this type of acting is a 'celibate man's' thing. Either way the heart is nowhere to be found. This is one good reason why women are needed in every level of church leadership. Women are much more in contact with the heart.

Religion is nothing if it does not enter the heart. Music is the helpmate. I wonder how many of you have 'celebrated' a Mass in a crowded church on Saturday or Sunday and there was no music? I attended a Christmas Morn Mass in a church in St. Charles County, MO that had no music, and no sign of peace. I felt like throwing up. I can only say I don't think the Spirit of God attended Mass that day.

The improvised music of Jazz and the Blues has an instinctive way of getting to the heart of those playing, and those hearing. This

---

[106] Ibid p. 26

music has the ability of dealing with the suffering, oppression, injustice, and violence of which our country is so much a part of today. Ann Peterson[107] writes, **"Music is a metaphor for learning to swing with grace under pressure"**. The grace come from God, the Spirit directs us to accomplish the works of God (beatitudes). Music is the energizer bunny.

An improvisational theology might well embrace the following 10 commandments:

1- A theology that embraces **revolution.**

2- A theology that believes that **all people** are created to God's Image.

3- A theology that builds on the **creativity and imagination** of God's People.

4- A theology that believes that the church is the **'People of God'**.

5- A theology that believes that humans are **created free** and that humans image God in the four dimensions - intellect - aesthetic - moral - spiritual.

6- A theology that reverences, admires, and **protects all of God's creation**.

7- A theology that **respects all religions**.

8- A theology that believes that God is **beyond all religions**.

9- A theology that believes that **faith is greater** than any dogma.

---

[107] Ibid p. 101

10- A theology that makes way for **human mistakes**.

"As Jesus was anointed Priest, Prophet, and King, so may you live always as a member of his body."

Baptism gives us power to sanctify, to teach, and to govern - Priesthood of the People

Recently in the United States we have had too many leaders who have not been Servant Leaders. Enron and Worldcom (to mention only 2) had leaders who were crooks and should be in prison. Because they are moneyed people they will probably will not see prison. They used; **secrecy** which always gives birth to the lie. **Patriarchy** was ever present as **dominators** and keeping women 'in their place'. They acted '**greater than**' the 'staff' and the stockholders appearing to be infallible. Also we are looking into the leadership style of our government as we became involved in our war against Iraq. We are seeing much of the same arrogance and secrecy as witnessed in business. However our political system has a built in **opposition party** which is supposed to take care of all that is unlawful and unethical within the government. However business and Church must rely on 'Whistle Blowers'.

The recent sexual scandal of the Catholic Church has only exposed the corrupt leadership style many church leaders have embraced. Even though our leaders no doubt have been acting in ignorance or innocence, this isn't to be considered **Servant Leadership**. One big difficulty here is a recent (1870) claim by the

Church of infallibility. **Infallibility** is acceptable when applied to God. Infallibility is very questionable when human beings get involved. With humans involved there needs to be some legal way of protecting 'whistle blowers', or their needs to be some legally established **Opposition Party** within the Church. Presently there are no checks and balances in the management of the church.

Infallibility is a cancer that has infected the leadership of the modern church. Where there are no 'checks and balances,' what gives control here is co-dependency. How it works is the people on the bottom of the ladder must give their obedience to their next power person along the hierarchichial set up. And this obedience must be blind for some leaders contend that we are obeying the *'will of God'*. The person who gives that blind obedience will be the one chosen to go to the next step of the ladder. There is great competition built into the system as one rises to the top. One who is not co-dependent will not advance to the top. A simple system that works but very vulgar of Human Dignity. All of this could be avoided, if the more traditional manner of the people electing their leaders would be adopted once again.

The weakness in all of this is **co-dependency. A co-dependent supports the addiction of their superior.** A co-dependent (the spouse of the alcoholic) becomes addicted to power (alcohol). The co-dependent does not think, does not create, and does not make decisions on their own, and does not correct or dissent. The co-dependent gives unmindful support for the addicted. The top person presumes everyone under him/her is co-dependent. In a situation as this often the leader gets ideas of grandeur and begins to think s/he is infallible, or that s/he is God, or both. Such a person is suffering with the addiction to Power, and their subjects have lapsed in to what Riane Eisler[108] calls the '**Dominator's Trance**'. With this in mind we have often heard the old saying (going back to 1870) **'Power corrupts and absolute power corrupts absolutely'**. It is a fail-safe system. History gives us hundreds of examples of this behavior in church and state.

Another grave defect is the present system of church leadership is the place of **women** in the institution. Or we may say there is no place for women in the leadership of the Catholic Church. From the very beginning (Genesis 1 & 2) women are equal and asked to be Co-creators with God in shaping the world. The absence of women in leadership is a monstrous evil.

The present church has reached global existence for the first time this century. It is a titanic responsibility. The desire of Jesus was to '**go to the whole world'**, but now that we are there we find that we **do not** have the leadership to accept this responsibility. The sexual scandal in USA shows how inadequate is the leadership style of the universal church. As a global church it will have to face the diversity of cultures, diversity of languages, the diversity of religions, the diversity of leadership styles in the world today. The present leadership style in our church today is not Servant Leadership. The

---

[108] Riane Eisler, "The Chalice & the Blade", Harper-SanFrancisco, 1995

vision and dream I have is that the Church of the future will drench itself in to the four dimensions of Aristotle:

—The Intellectual is nourished by Truth. There will be Servant Leadership of the church, it will concern itself with truth and will gain the trust of the People of God. This leadership will give up its addiction to power, and escape from patriarchy. As leaders of truth and trust there will be no more need to use deception or manipulation. Change along with chaos will be expected and greeted. Leadership will lead in the belief that all men and women of the world are created equal and to the Image of God.

—The Aesthetic is directed toward Beauty. Leadership will encourage the God given gifts of creativity and imagination of the People of God. Leadership will recognize the amazing gifts of the feminine, and will accept networking among all religions. The beautiful diversity of God's creation will be celebrated and preserved. Aesthetics conquers passivity in ritual (liturgy) while it encourages faith on fire.

—The Moral is attracted to Goodness. Servant Leadership will promote prophecy in bringing moral goodness to our world. The human being is respected and develops moral integrity in an atmosphere of freedom, and in the framework of law. We take a serious look at the morality of the developing franchise parish (as business), and ask, "Is this moral?". Leadership will revise Canon Law to bring it in conformity to the law of Jesus **'Love the Neighbor as oneself.'**

—The Spiritual generates Unity. Spirituality of a Servant leader engenders unity among religions, which in turn brings peace. Spirituality will bring unity where there is diversity, and acceptance where there is uniqueness. The servant leader encourages tolerance, justice, and acceptance within a plurality of people worldwide. The end work of spirituality is living as community. Finally the spirituality of gentleness and forgiveness will make servant leader's work the work of God.

One final note - James Caroll[109] a theologian and a married priest speaks of the necessity of calling Vatican III. When this council is called I hope it will be in Manila or Kampala rather than at the Vatican. The Curia needs not to be in control. Carroll sets out 5 needs to be discussed and dialogued. 1. To have a **biblical literacy** - This is what Martin Luther looked for, and this was one hope of Vatican II. 2. The church needs to deal with the question of **Power** and how it is used or abused, especially infallibility. 3. With the biblical literacy, we need a **new Christology**. 4. Something he calls the **'Holiness of Democracy'**, and certainly Jesus did not forbid democracy, nor did he forbid the inclusion of women. 5. A definite **call for repentance**, especially with our various different religions around the world. Wars will be stopped when we look upon our non-catholic religions as friends rather than enemies.

I simply state that Leadership in the church is of extreme importance now and forever. There are many things happening today

---

[109] James Carroll, "Toward a New Catholic Church", Houghton Mifflin Co. Boston, 2002

in the church that indicates that Servant Leadership is needed. The next council will have to spend a great deal of time looking into the style of leadership that Jesus devised -**Servant Leadership.**

Bibliography

America, 30 July - August 6 2001,

America, Robert Kress, "The Priest-Pastor As C.E.O.", March 11, 2

America, Francis A. Sullivan S.J. "The Magisterium in the New Millennium", August 27-September 3, 2001

Eugene C. Bianchi, "A democratic Catholic Church", (Crossroad, New York, 1992)

Walter Brueggmann, "Hopeful Imagination", Fortress Press, Philadelphia, 1986

National Catholic Reporter, Gary MacEoin, "Seeds of the Word", Feb. 8, 2000

James Carroll, "Toward a New Catholic Church", Houghton Mifflin Co. Boston, 2002

Carter, Stephen L. (Basic Books; 10 E. 53rd St. N.Y. 1998)

Deepak Chopra, "How to know God", Three Rivers Press, NY, 2000

Riane Eisler, "The Chalice & the Blade", Harper San Francisco, CA.1988

Raymond Flynn, "The Accidental Pope", St. Martin's Press, NY, 2000.

Marion M. Forst, "Daily Journal of Vatican II", Forest of Peace Pub. Kansas City, KS, 2000

Matthew Fox, "The Reinvention of Work" Harper, San Francisco, 1994

Samuel Fromartz, St. Louis Post, Section C5, Monday May 5, 2003

Joel Garreau, "Washington Post National Weekly" August 20-26, 2001

Joseph Girzone, "Joshua" or "Joshua and the City" or "Joshue and the Children", Image Books, NY. 1995, 1998

Elllen Goodman St Louis Post Dispatch, "What shadows hide", Sunday March 10, 2002

Roger Haight, "Jesus Symbol of God", Orbis Press, NY 2000 p. 37-39

Thich Nhat Hanh, "Old Path White Clouds: Walking in the Footsteps of the Buddha" Berkeley, CA 1991

Chris Hedges, "War is a Force That GIves Us Meaning"Public Affairs, New YOrk, 2002,

William L. Forst

William R. Herzog II, "Jesus, Justice, Reign of God", Westminister John Knox Press, Louisville, KY, 2000,

Abraham Heschel, 'The Prophets: an Introduction", Harper and Row, NY, 1962

Olwen Hufton; "The Prospect Before Her", (Alfred A. Knope, N.Y.) 1996

Elizabeth A. Johnson editor, Diana Hayes, "The Church Women Want", Crossroads Pub Co. NY.2002

Roger Karban, "Jesus and Community", Victorious Missinoaries, Belleville, IL

Mary Kenny, "Goodbye to Catholic Ireland", Templegate Pub. Springfield IL, 2000,

Ursula King, "Spirit of Fire", (Orbis Books, New York, 10545, 1998)

Kuhnts, "Structure of Scientific Revolution", Phoenix Books, University of Chicago, 1 962

Hans Kung, "A Global Ethic for Global Politics and Economics", Oxford University Press, NY 1998

Chung Hyun Kyung, "Struggle to be the Sun Again", Orbis Books, Maryknkoll, N.Y. 1990

Lawrence LeShan, 'The Psychology of War" Helios, New York, 1992

Lipnack, J. & Stamps, J. "The Networking Book", Routledge and Kegan Paul. 1986

Megan McKenna, "The Prophet", Orbis Books, NY, 2001

Margaret Meadows, "Whole Earth Models and Systems."Co-Evolution Quarterly (Summer 1982):

Christian Science Monitor, August 10, 1998, B1

Christina Science Monitor, Mark Clayton, "Scandals will dent, not bankrupt, dioceses." March 28, 2002

Christian Science Monitor, "Scandals will dent, not bankrupt, dioceses," By Mark Clayton, March 28, 2002

Friedrich Nietzsche, "A Nietzsche Reader", 221, 217-18: Aphorisms from Daybreak,

Diarmuid O'Murchu, "Reclaiming Spirituality", Crossroad Pub Co., New York, 1999

Ann Peterson, "God, Creation, and all that Jazz", Chalice Press, St. Louis MO.2001

Hermann J. Pottmeyer, 'Towards a Papacy in Communion;—" New York, Herder/Crossroads, 1998

John R. Quinn, "The Reform of the Papacy:—" Herder/Crossraods, NY, 1999

Also Larry Rasmussen, "Shaping Communities," Ed. Dorothy C. Bass, (San Francisco: Jossey-Bass, 1997) 121

Rachel Naomi Remen, M.D. "Kitchen Table Wisdom", Riverhead Books, NY, 1996

Cokie Roberts, "We are Our Mothers' Daughters", (William Morrow & Co. N.Y.) 1998

Daniel N. Robinson, "The Great Ideas of Philosophy", Georgetown University, The Teaching Company,

St. Louis Post, Rachel Melcher, Section 3, Pages 1 & 5, Monday May 5, 2003

St. Louis Post Dispatch, News, Friday June 14, 2002

St. Louis Post Dispatch, Kevin Horrigan, "A '50s priesthood lost—", 3/10/02

St. Louis Post Dispatch, Carey, Christopher, "Business Ethics", January 6, 2002, B1

St. Louis Post-Dispatch, Thomas Friedman. copyrighted from New York Times, November 29, 2001

St. Louis Post Dispatch, Molly Mins, "The Solution To Our Problems: LIE", Editorial, Friday June 27, 2003 - Copyright Creators Syndicate

St. Louis Post Dispatch, Paige Byrne Shortal, "Whose sin is it? Society?" March 12, 2002 Metro

Eric Schlosser, "Fast Food Nation", Houghton Mifflin Co. New York, 2001

Sandra M. Schneiders, "Written That You May Believe" Herder And Herder NY, 1999

Sandra M. Schneiders, "Finding the Treasure", Paulist Press, NY, 2000bc, p.354

Bennett J. Sims, "Servanthood", (Cowley Publications, Cambridge MA.1997)

Swidler, Leonard, "Toward a Catholic Constitution", (Crossroad Pub Co. N.Y.) 1996

William L. Forst

Brian Swimme and Thomas Berry, "The universe Story", (San Francisco: HarperCollins, 1992),
Simone Weil, 'The Lliad' or 'The Poem of Force', "Wallingford, PA; Pendle Hill Pamphlet, 1993,
Margaret J. Wheately, "Leadership and the New Science". Berrett-Koehler Pubs. San Francisco, 1999
Garry Wills, "Papal Sin" (Doubleday, NY) 2000
Richard Woods, "The Seven Bowls of Wrath: An Ecological Parable," Ecotheology 7 (1999)
Gary Zukav, "Soul Stories", Simon & Schuster, NY, 2000

Index

2 Cor 3:17, 83
2 Thess 5:19, 2
Absolute power, x, 12, 13, 17, 27, 124, 149
Acts 1:25, 16
Acts 10:34, 14, 92, 117
Acts 13:26-27, 79
Acts 15:22, 58
Acts 9:15, 84
Aesthetics, xiii, 3, 45, 50, 54, 57, 62, 70, 150
Africa, viii, 119
African Americans, 112
Amos 6:1-7, 114
Aquinas, Thomas, 8, 21, 22, 26, 45, 53, 65
Arch, 48
Arian heresy, 35
Aristotle, xii, xiii, xiv, 1, 6, 15, 20, 22, 27, 34, 40, 53, 58, 62, 65, 70, 74, 75, 87, 103, 106, 123, 128, 142, 150
Armenian, 118
Assisi, Francis, 53
Athenagoras, 104
Autopoiesis, 5, 6
Ava, MO, 46
Balasuriya, Tissa, 89, 125
Baltimore Catechism, 54
Baptism, 16, 64, 84, 118, 147
Berry, Thomas, 104, 156
Birth Control, 19, 31, 32
Bosnia, 78, 115
Bramante, 48
Brewer, Jerry, 55

Brezezinski, Zbigniew, 75
Buddhist, 42, 52, 76, 112
Burger King, 93
Byzantine, 118
Caesaro-Papism, 65, 84
Canon Law, 32, 94, 99, 102, 150
Carroll, Bishop John, 39
Carter, Stephen, 123
Caste system, 2, 4, 58, 59, 60, 119
Casti Connubi, 31
Catholic Charities, viii, 120
Chaardin, Fr. Teilhard de, 39
Chaldean, 118
chaos, 5, 6, 49, 50, 90, 125, 150
Chiapas, Mexico, 81
Chopra, Deepak, 107, 153
Cicero, xii
Collegiality, 60
Confucius, xii, 3, 9, 74
Constantine, 21, 23, 58, 64, 102
Coptic, 118
Cosmic Christ, 104
Council of Trent, 3, 65, 143
Creativity-Imagination, 50
Crusades, 14, 84
Curia, 18, 19, 20, 37, 42, 51, 61, 87, 125, 134, 151
Curran, Charles, 89
Dallas TX, 11
Danneels, Cardinal, 48
Darwin, 34

De Chardin, Teilhard, 50, 69, 117
Democracy, 151
Democratic, 6, 15, 16, 20, 31, 39, 40, 58, 153
Descartes, Rene, 70
Diesel, Rudolf C., 52
Diogenes, 26
Dominguez, Elizabeth, 137
duality, 107, 108
Edict of Milar, x, 64
Einstein, 34
Einstein, Albert, 78, 141
Eisler, Riane, 57, 149, 153
Ekklesia, 40
England, Bishop John, 39
Enron, 26, 76, 147
Eph 4:11, 79
Equality, 40
Ethics, 74, 75, 76, 155
Ethics Officers, 75
Ethiopian, 118
Fast Food Nation, 47, 92, 155
Feminine, 62, 70
Ford, Henry, 34
Forst, Bishop Marion, 86, 153
Fox, Matthew, 124, 140, 153
Franchise, 91, 92
Franchise Parish, 91
Franklin, Benjamin, 52
Freedom – Moral Act, 83
Friedman, Thomas, 116, 155
Gal 3:27-28, 41
Gal 5:14, 107
Gal 5:18, 14, 97, 100
Galations 5:13, 83
Galileo, 34, 89, 124
Galvini, Luigi, 52

Gebrara, Ivone, 1, 49
Gen 1:27, 90
Gen 2:23, 125
General Motors, xiv, 2, 33, 42, 113, 124, 132, 142
Genesis 1 & 2, 149
Global, xv, 71, 154
Globalization, 36
Goddess, 57
Goodman, Ellen, 28
Gregory, Bishop Wilton, 11
Griffith, Bishop James, 86
Grimby Pizza, 93
Gulf War, 140
Haight, Fr. Roger, 56, 115
Han Kuk Yum, 25
Haring, Bernard, 89
Harman, Willis, 138
Harris, Joseph C., 96
Hayes, Diana, 88, 154
Hebrew Bible, 21, 70
Hedges, Chris, 29, 30, 153
Herzog, William, 23, 154
Heschel, Rabbi Abraham, 80
Hispanics, 112
Hoge, Dean, 96
Horrigan, Kevin, 29, 155
House Churches, 64
HUD, 97
Hufton, Olwen, 66, 154
Human Dignity, 90, 148
Humanae Vitae, 30, 32
I Thess 5:19, 50
Inculteration, 36, 120
Islamic, 52
Jantsch, 90
Jefferson, Thomas, 110
Jn 13:13-15, 18

Jn 13:35, 135
Jn 15:15, 129
Jn 17:17, 8
Jn 18:37, 2
Jn 3:8, 51
Jn 4:3-42, 63
Jn 6:60-67, 12
Jn 7:52, 79
Jn 8:32, 36
Jn 9:1-41, 116
Johnson, Sr. Elizabeth, 20
Kampala, 109, 151
Karban, Fr. Roger, 134
Katoppo, Marianne, 24
Kenny, Mary, 32, 154
King, Martin L. Jr., 77, 87
Kress, Robert, 95, 153
Kuhnts, 49, 154
Kung, Fr. Hans, 111
Kung, Hans, 71, 89, 154
Lenehan, Catherine, 67
LeShan, Lawrence, 29, 154
Levi Strauss Co., 75
Lin Yutang, 45
Lipnack & Stamps, 61
Lk 12:49, 57
Lord Acton, 12, 13
Louise de Marillac, 66
Luther, Martin, 56, 77, 87, 89, 124, 142, 151
MacEoin, Gary, 81, 119, 153
Malcom X, 85
Marcuse, Herbert, 74, 110
Mark 12:28-34, 99
Maronite, 118
Mary Magdalyn, 64
Mary –Mother of Jesus, 24, 62, 70

Matthias, 16
Mayan, 81, 82
McDonald-Douglas Co, 140
McKenna, Megan, 79, 80, 154
Meadows, Donella, 4
Medina, Cardinal, 19
Micah 4:1-4, 77
Michelangelo, 48
Mins, Molly, 27, 155
Mirari vos, 38
misbegotten male, 21, 59, 62
Mk 8:18, 123
Modern World, 74, 85, 89
Mosaic Law, 102
Mother Theresa, 67
Mt 13:57, 79
Mt 20:25, 9
Mt 23:5-11, 15
Mt 7:4-5, 34
Mt. 5:17, 79
Murray, Fr. John C, 38, 87
Murray, John C., 38, 87
Nasca, 120
National Parishes, 112
Networking, 57, 59, 60, 61, 154
New Oxford Review, 95
Newton, Isaac, 3, 70
Newtonian, 5, 6, 34, 103
Nichting, Sylvan & Joan, 50
Nietzsche, 12, 13, 154
Northern Ireland, 78, 115
Novo Millennio, 133
Otto, Nick, 52
Out of Box, 55
Paine, Thomas, 1
Patriarchy, 20, 24, 25, 37, 147
Persian Gulf War, 30

Peru, viii, 95, 120
Philippines, 137
Phoebe, 64
Pneuma, 50, 51, 72
Pope Gregory XVI, 38
Pope John XXIII, x, 31, 37, 102
Pope Paul VI, 30, 78, 104, 109, 119
Pope Pius IX, 4
Pope Urban VIII, 66
Power-with, 131
Pregogin & Stengers, 33
Printing Press, 36
Prisca & Aquila, 64
Prodigal Son, 53
Prophecy, 77
Protestant Reform, 3
Psalm 34:13, 27
Quantum physics, 4
Rapheal, 48
Rassmussen, Larry, 137
Religious Freedom, 38, 85, 86, 87
Remen, Rachel, 105
restorationists, 35
Reuter, Mary Lea Pneuma, 55
Richard, Pablo, 119
Rigali, Archbishop, 95
Rm 14:12, 85
Rm 2:11, 14, 92
Rm 8:21, 2
Roberts, Cokie, 67, 155
Rom 11:13, 52
Rom 12:6-8, 121
Rom 16, 64
Rom 16:1, 64
Roosevelt, Franklin D., 17

Rosell, Mark, 28
Ruiz, Bishop Samuel, 81
Ryan, Michael W., 95
Saarinen, Ero, 48
Samaritan Woman, 53
Savanarola, 89
Scandal of 2002, 7
Schlosser, Eric, 47, 92, 155
Schneiders, Sr. Sandra, 21, 126, 135
Scholasticism, 65
Self-organizing, 90
self-reference, 90, 91
Self-referencing, 5, 90
Sheldrake, Rupert, 141
Shupe, Anson, 94
Sims, Bishop Bennett, 133
Sisters of Charity, 66
Socrates, xii, 20, 77
Spellman, Cardinal, 38
Spillane, Mary Beth, 47
St. Charles County, 113, 145
St. Jerome, 66
St. Steven, 84
Subsidiarity, xi, 60
Swidler, Leonard, 38
Swimme, Brian, 104, 156
Syrian, 118
Taliban, 69, 116
Temple, 23
Terence, 97, 102
Thich Nhat Hanh, 42, 153
Tonkin Gulf, 27
Torah, 99
Trade Center, 108, 115
Trappist, 46
Twain, Mark, 27
United Nations, 77, 78

Unity as uniqueness, 117
US Constitution, 35, 36, 87, 110
Vatican Council I, 4, 13, 16, 60, 74
Vatican Council II, 4, 16, 60, 74
Vatican Council II Laity, 16, 17
Vatican II, x, 6, 7, 16, 26, 31, 35, 37, 38, 55, 68, 85, 86, 89, 104, 109, 119, 120, 131, 133, 143, 151, 153
Vatican Museum, 48
Vladimiroff, Sr. Christine, 18

WACs, 67
Wash Feet, ix, x, xiii, 7, 18, 130, 132
Washing Feet, 18, 129
Washington Post, 54, 153
WAVEs, 67
Weakland, 19
Weil, Simone, 30, 113, 114, 156
Wheatley, Margaret, 42, 90, 91
Wills, Gary, 29
Wright, Bishop John, 86
WWJD, 76, 114
Zukav, Gary, 10, 156

About the Author

Bill Forst was born in 1928 in St. Louis, MO. He has parents who by their love for each other and their expressed love for justice taught him how to be a priest. He has learned a great deal about leadership by being the youngest of four girls and four boys, the oldest being a Bishop and the middle brother a Monsignor and five being married.

Bill was ordained a priest April of 1954 with a class of 30. After two years he found himself in the Jefferson City Diocese, which was newly created from the St. Louis Diocese. As a priest he feels very blessed with the many varied tasks to which he was assigned.

He was assistance, then pastor, studied for a MEd in Secondary school Administration. He was then appointed Principal of the new St. Thomas Seminary, Hannibal. His task was to have the school accredited. He was vocation Director, later founder and co-director of Social Concerns (Catholic Charities). He then volunteered for the Diocesan Missions in Peru. Later Bill was assigned to Team Ministry in three counties of Northern Missouri. Then he worked for several years in the State Prison system, and finally spent a number of years in Hospital ministry. With each task the priesthood was enlivened. He is a man of great leadership experience. Gradually, with each priestly experience, Bill found himself quite different from his Bishop and some priests of his diocese. He is a priest of hope, and he believes the church will change its present leadership style to the servant leadership advocated by Jesus.

Printed in the United States
20677LVS00003B/361